Scenes From A Life Well Lived

by Joe Mara

Editor: Sean Hillen
Book design: Columbia Hillen

'Joe Will Be Remembered By Learned Words'

On December 12, 2020 at 6:50 p.m. the seven-word message above suddenly appeared on my cell phone. There was no name or number with it. Then it disappeared. I could not find it anywhere no matter how hard I tried.

At that time, Joe, my beloved husband, was in the hospital on a ventilator. He passed away four days later.

Joe, 67, was born in Dublin, Ireland in March, 1953, moved to England to join his family in 1957 and finally arrived on America's shores in 1979 where we met two years later at a sock hop in a Wall Street N.Y. area loft.

At that time, after graduating from Hull College in England, Joe's focus was on film-making and he freelanced in the industry building sets, then progressed into writing and making short films.

He then became an educator, teaching video and art in New York's public school system. He obtained his Masters' degree in writing which subsequently became his passion in life. He wrote columns for our local newspaper '*The Wave*' which became very popular.

Many people would stop me to ask if Joe Mara the columnist was the same Joe I was married to. He always managed to capture everyone's attention with his stories and good humor.

Joe taught at Bank Street College, Bard Summer Academy and the Children's Museum of Manhattan. He was also a video artist in residency at the Professional Performing Arts School and the School of Science and Technology in Manhattan and ran a Teacher's Media Center where teachers were taught how to use video technology in the classroom.

Life is a struggle, but Joe was a determined man and one of his long-held goals was to write a book. But death came too quickly and he never got to finish the task he had set himself. Here, however, is Joe's memoir, from childhood to his later years, providing a glimpse into the ups and downs of his life, his beliefs and his enduring sense of humor that helped him to the very end.

Joe was a tolerant, humble, genuine and knowledgeable guy. He taught me the beauty of the sky at night, in particular Venus, which we would gaze at sitting on our front porch whenever it appeared.

I learned about art, history, fables, film,

humour, culture, family life and even death from him. Joe was a well-rounded person who knew much about life in general and was always so willing to share information.

Joe is missed very much by me, his family and all his friends.

I think it right and fitting to end this tribute to Joe by quoting from one of his favorite books, '*A Tale of Two Cities*' by Charles Dickens, '*It is a far, far better thing that I do, than I have ever done; it is a far, far better rest I go to than I have ever known.*'

Joe's loving wife, forever.
Roe Mara

Joe Mara - A Lover Of Words

Sadly, I didn't have the pleasure of meeting Joe Mara in person but we 'met' so many times as fellow travellers wandering together through the world of words that I feel I knew him well.

When my wife, Columbia and I at 'Ireland Writing Retreat' organised our inaugural 'Wild Atlantic Writing Awards,' Joe was among the first to enter his work. That began our journey together, he asking me if I would read his manuscript about his life and the lives of his Irish-born parents.

That's how I learned more about the kind of man Joe was, his passion for story-telling, his love of reading and his deep-felt need to present to the world a portrait of his family and of his growing up in Ireland and England in the '60s and '70s.

Joe dearly wanted his memoir to be part of his lasting legacy, and I promised Roe, his loving wife, that her dear husband would not be forgotten, that I would help share his memory with others, some of whom themselves may have faced heart-breaking personal loss in their lives.

So, reading this right now, consider yourself among Joe's friends. Take a moment to enjoy his obvious delight in words and stories and visualise what a warm and convivial character he was.

And, please, make sure you don't hesitate to write your own story.

Heed Chaucer's famous words, '*Time and tide wait for no man.*'

Sean Hillen
Author, Editor, Publisher and Tutor at Ireland
Writing Retreat
(irelandwritingretreat.com)

Scenes From A Life Well Lived

DEATH COMES SUDDEN,
SOMETIMES

The phone rang. It was evening, the Sunday after Christmas. It was my oldest brother Dave calling from England.

"It's kind of late over there isn't it Dave?" my wife, Roe, asked.

My good humour changed to dread as she handed me the phone.

You never know when you're going to get the call. About a friend, a parent, a loved one. But sooner or later we all get them. As you get older, they become more frequent.

"It's Daddy Joe....he's been in hospital... tonight...he had a ..."

"Is he dead?" I asked, instantly knowing the answer.

"Yes."

It's not fair. I thought. Retired in October, dead

in December. He had just flown over with Mum from Ireland to spend Christmas with his sons and grandchildren. And now, at 73, he was gone.

1987 had not ended well.

UNITED IN GRIEF

I made arrangements to be in London the next day.

Just like that, time, money and work suddenly no object. A thought crossed my mind. I wished arrangements could be made as easily when people were still alive.

My second eldest brother, Tim, came on the phone and we commiserated. Ever the philosopher, he said, "It's been a helluva day here Joe. Could we have done something differently? Could we have got him to the hospital sooner? Would it have changed anything? But you know Joe, it's not like a videotape, we can't replay it or change anything. He's just gone, and that's that."

My two brothers met me at Heathrow. In the car going through London I tried to learn more about Dad's death. He'd been complaining all weekend about not feeling well. Stomach pains. They'd become so bad my brothers had taken him to Whipps

3

Cross Hospital in northeast London. There he was diagnosed with a stomach aneurysm. While he was waiting for an operation the aneurysm burst. And that was the end of him.

Our conversation drifted on to details about the nightmarish scene that awaited them at Whipps Cross. As they waited for Dad to have his operation, the hospital had become rowdier as English yobs, drunks and stab-wound victims poured in after closing time at the pubs. It wasn't a pleasant sight. Dave swore he never wanted to see the inside of Whipps Cross Hospital again. Unfortunately for him, he broke his leg two years later skiing in France and found himself in the very same ward as Dad.

By all accounts, my family had enjoyed a wonderful Christmas together. They'd played charades and Trivial Pursuit with their grandchildren. Their stay had been a lot of fun. Now, suddenly it was all over.

As our car journey continued, we regaled each other with memories of Dad.

"A funny bloke, wasn't he?" Dave mused. "Didn't really want much, did he? Or need much."

Light-hearted stories helped lighten our mood.

His legendary cheapness, for example, to the point of eccentricity. I recalled one Christmas, too cheap to buy a plastic Christmas tree, he'd chopped down a lemon tree in our garden, decorating it nicely with traditional lights. Our neighbours were delighted, the English being somewhat eccentric too.

Or the time he used to send away for free

sample design books. And how he'd paste plain white
discounted rolls of wallpaper in our rooms, then add
his very own design to them by cutting out pieces
from one of his sample books. Our bedrooms soon
reflected their own peculiar style, red roses glued on
to white paper in random fashion. When I was about
fifteen, I borrowed his idea, cutting out nude pictures
from an art book and pasting them cleverly on to the
roses. For a while, Dad didn't even notice. When
finally he did, he simply commented dryly, "Very
funny."

Dad even encased photos of our treasured
childhood in a most idiosyncratic manner - inside
clothing and wallpaper catalogues he'd gotten free.
So, alongside photos of us in the 'albums,' there were
illustrations of women in '50s style outfits - long
dresses with tight belts and men wearing what
appears now to be utterly ridiculous shoes. There we
were, our childhood sandwiched between shoes and
cheap wallpaper.

Upon seeing these family heirlooms, an artist
friend was momentarily stunned. Then declared
admiringly, "These are pop art masterpieces."

Then there was the memorable occasion in a
bar in America on my Dad's last trip to visit us. I
preface this anecdote by saying that Dad was not a
big drinker. In fact, he frowned upon people who
allowed themselves to get drunk. Everything he did
was in moderation. He went to church every Sunday
and believed quite simply there was a God, who was
probably Catholic, and a heaven and a hell, a good

and an evil. Accordingly, every day he made moral decisions about what was right and what was wrong. To him, life was simple. If everyone followed the Christian message of 'charity for all,' the world would be a much better place.

But on the last night of his American visit, between drinking at home and socialising at our local bar, I suddenly realised the man with the moderating philosophy was indeed quite drunk. I knew this because I had to grab him by the scruff of his neck as he almost tottered downstairs, keen to go to another bar at midnight.

I couldn't believe it, it was the first time I'd ever seen him even slightly inebriated. At the bar, everyone started buying Dad drinks. He was a novelty. Unlike them, he was authentically Irish, an amusing little fellow all the way from the Auld Sod. As the night wore on Dad became ever more animated, so much so my Mum suddenly dared him to dance an Irish Jig with a young girl at the bar who thought he was cute. Much to our amazement, this normally intensely shy man stood up and proceeded to dance energetically with the attractive girl. Everybody thought it was great fun until he overreached himself and careened into the jukebox, immediately disrupting the music. It was then Dad decided it was time to go home.

The next morning at breakfast, he really did look badly hung-over.

"How's your head, Dad?" I asked.

"Fine. Why?"

"Well, you really tied one on last night."

"What do you mean?" he answered, all innocent looking, his face an expression of denial.

I said nothing further, deciding to let him have his secret pleasure. My brothers, however, gasped in astonishment when I told them.

"You mean the old fella was drunk? Really drunk?"

"Yes," I replied. "Shit-faced. Pissed. Stoned. Out of his box. Out of his brains." They simply couldn't believe it.

I've often wondered why this had happened. I think it was because my Dad knew time was running out. He'd religiously restrained himself all his life so probably thought God wouldn't mind him having a few too many pints just this once with his son in America.

My Dad loved America. He'd always been intrigued by it, or rather the idea of it. When I was a kid, one of my favorite books was, 'The Travels of Marco Polo' which he'd given me to read. Dad shared a childlike fascination about a man who'd gone to a land, China, that nobody in the West knew about, a man who'd returned home with tales of a place where people made fires from a black substance in the earth called coal and who ate a strange food called rice which grew in waterlogged fields.

Dad said when I was older we'd travel all over the world together like Marco Polo. But in all Dad's twenty years in England, he'd never been further north than Wolverhampton, 140 miles away where my brother Tim went to college. So, when he finally came to New York, he was ecstatic. He'd finally been somewhere. And New York wasn't just anywhere. In a way, it was 'the world' to him.

PAINTING A RAINBOW

After a few hours, my brothers and I finally arrived in South Woodford, northeast London, where Dave lived and where Mum and Dad had been staying over Christmas. My other brother Charlie, his wife Janet and their 10-year-old daughter Charlotte were there too, having travelled up from Kent.

My Mum was still in a state of shock as she walked down the stairs to greet me. She looked exactly as you'd expect anyone to look under the circumstances, utterly frazzled. While it had been left unsaid, it was always expected Dad would go first because he was the frailer of the two.

I thought at worst it might be a slow, lingering death from cancer because of chain-smoking unfiltered cigarettes most of his life, which left the fingers of his right hand nicotine-brown and he had developed emphysema within the last year. Indeed, there in the living-room, was his unopened carton of duty-free cigarettes, a Christmas tree spookily towering over them.

The next day our extended family, including sons, wives and nieces, flew to Dublin. As black was the current fashion trend in England, my teenage nieces, Tim and Belinda's daughters, Alice and Emily, didn't have to adjust their funeral clothes much. My oldest brother, Dave, who hates flying, had somehow finagled an Aer Lingus stewardess to give him a strong shot of Irish whiskey.

After take-off, Alice of the flaming red hair, and flaming wit, said, "What if this plane crashes? It would be a whole generation of Maras gone, the headlines would read, `Mara, Mara, Mara, Mara, Mara, Mara, Mara, Mara, Mara, killed in plane crash.'"

Dave just groaned and gulped down his whiskey.

Later that evening we went to the funeral home. The scene looked somehow unreal. Dad's body lay in a closed coffin and people came to pay their respects. It was the first time I had seen the coffin and it seemed eerie to me. Like it had come from outer space and had just landed, with my Dad inside. The spell was broken when one of my aunts began frantically to chant the rosary. Everyone joined in. All those Sunday masses, altar boy training and Catechism lessons suddenly returned at once, shocking me all over again.

That night our motorcade procession made its way to Dublin where the funeral mass and burial were to take place. Dad's hearse led the way. As we passed the Gresham Hotel where my parents had stayed after they were married, I wondered what Mum was thinking. A sad and teary mood overcame me at the thought of it. As we gazed at the hearse ahead of us, Tim, ever the wag, parted the dark clouds, saying, "Do you think Daddy would have liked going through Dublin feet first?"

The next day was the funeral mass. My brother Charlie, a strait-laced banker, had organised the details, including funeral arrangements and interment, like a military-style operation. Hence, he'd been dubbed 'The Commander' by the rest of us. Two priests officiated, as well as a Bishop, my Mum's cousin, Bobby Jones.

I remembered Bobby as a kid. He was a lot of fun, a golf nut who'd bring his clubs everywhere including my Uncle Eamon's farm in County Meath and practice his swings on acres of land. He let us take some swings too. But later, after he became a priest, he struck me as being unctuous and I didn't have much time for him anymore.

Now he was a Bishop, giving a eulogy for Dad, which I hadn't been expecting. He started by saying Dad, "hadn't painted the world rainbow colours."

To me, Dad had painted the world rainbow colours and I was beginning to get annoyed with Bobby all over again. He continued, describing a long bike-ride he and Dad had taken in their teens to southern Wicklow, the next county over from Dublin. He described it joyfully as two young men taking a trip, "a long time ago before the world got so busy, like it is today." I suddenly realised these men had been really good friends in their youth. He continued in this vein giving a simple but heartfelt account of Dad, using their long ago friendship as a touchstone. It was a very fine eulogy indeed, capturing the essence of their friendship in a touching way. I began liking Bobby Jones again.

After Mass was over and everything had gone exactly to Charlie's plan, we all hung around waiting to go to the cemetery. Initially, there were about 200 people, now all that was left were family members and close friends and we were all chatting informally. But the best laid plans of mice and men, and bankers, can sometimes go astray.

Above the congenial hubbub, a loud voice was suddenly heard. "I can raise him," it said. "I can raise this man from the dead."

Tim later said he thought a `fearful Jesuit' had gotten into the place. Everybody turned and there, up on the altar beside Dad's coffin, stood a long-haired, deranged man speaking in a clear British accent. England's revenge personified.

"I can raise this man from the dead, I have the power but you must believe," he said.

The church fell silent. My brother Charlie, incensed, rushed up to the altar and grabbed the man. I joined him immediately and we frog-marched the stranger out of the church.

The man continued to rant and rave and Charlie, normally the gentlest of men, was ready to hit him. He'd spoilt everything. I had worked in a mental health clinic in New York so was used to this kind of situation. In fact, the stranger even looked a lot like one of my clients.

"Charlie, he's crazy, let him go." And he did.

BACK TO WHERE IT ALL BEGAN

Why had England 'taken revenge' on Dad in this way at his own funeral? Was it because he'd espoused contempt for the country during the first years he'd lived there after leaving Ireland?

For answers, let's go back in time.

Both my parents were pharmacists and had owned a string of chemist shops in Dublin. Then their business went bust. So, in 1956 they went to England, desperately looking for work. From business owners, they now had to work for other people and due to the political relationship between England and Ireland, their Irish chemistry degrees weren't even recognised. This meant they had lower jobs and salaries than they deserved considering their qualifications and years of experience. Combined with the typical Irish indignation with the English, this resentment bitterly manifested itself in a constant barrage of anti-English talk.

Such was the height of Dad's contempt when England played Germany in the final of the World Cup in 1966, he brainwashed us to root for Germany, probably the only house in the entire country that did so. He'd exclaim about the English players, "Have you ever seen such a lucky team in your life? And that Gordon Banks' save against Pele, supposedly the greatest ever, don't believe it. It was a lucky touch and the English will still be talking about it in a hundred years even though they lost the match."

So, while the rest of the nation went crazy when England won, we were left crushed. Suddenly, more than ever before, we understood we were foreigners in a strange land.

My older brother Tim can't escape some responsibility for the situation that played out in our house through the summer of 1966. At sixteen he'd met an English girl on a school trip to Germany. She was a schoolmate's sister who happened to live in Munchengladbach because her dad worked at the army base there. He fell madly in love, as teenagers do, and had gone back several times. My parents grumbled but he told them he was going to her parents' house, on an army base in Germany, so what could happen? Not only were there stars in his eyes when he'd return from but he was also taken with Germany itself, which was utter heresy in England at the time.

There was still tremendous animosity, even sheer hatred, towards the Germans, mostly from the older generation who'd been through the war. But

Tim spoke of a Germany that seemed intact and prosperous compared to England. It had been quickly rebuilt under the Marshall Plan, mainly by the Americans, and was thriving. Tim told us of the incredible food he'd had - wieners, schnitzels and wursts. And as much as you wanted, unlike stingy England. Also, there were fabulous bierkellers and a throbbing nightlife that he downplayed with my parents, but not with us. It seemed the poor shagged-out England we now lived in had won the War but the Germans had definitely won the peace.

But no matter what happened, we still couldn't support England because, first and foremost, we were Irish. Our connection with Ireland was strong. All our cousins, uncles and aunts were back in Ireland. Ritually, every summer, we'd all head back there. We brothers would bring in the hay on one of my uncles' farms. With our funny English accents, our relatives considered us 'the Lost Tribe.' We were English in Ireland, and Irish in England.

Every year, as we approached the headland of Ireland on the ferry, we all knew we were going home, back to our other lives, which had been so diabolically snatched from us. Every St. Patrick's Day, Dad got a huge shamrock package from Ireland and made sure we all wore a bunch on our lapels. When we got to school, the few other Irish kids and ourselves were taunted ad nauseam by the English kids 'for wearing weeds, grass and bog flowers' on our jackets.' By the age of fifteen, I would wear my shamrock as I went out of the house, but took it off once I got to school. About the same time, I started skipping mass whenever I could. Sorry Dad, England was calling me. But rest easy, it never replaced Ireland.

Once, during a debate in our English class, a subject was suggested by the worst anti-Irish kid. It was entitled, 'Irish people still live in bogs and are not as advanced as the English.' Now one should keep in mind that for centuries the Irish have been the butt of ethnic jokes in England about their stupidity and drunkenness. Being a brain-washed Irish patriot via my Dad, I was induced to argue the opposing viewpoint and thus avenge centuries of enforced cultural inferiority.

My Dad pointed out that all the great English statesmen were Irish anyway. People like Wellington and Montgomery. Furthermore, as the greatest writers in the world were Irish, Joyce and Shaw were to be included in my frontal assault on the insulting English. I was also told to mention the great Irish religious and cultural renaissance beginning with St. Kevin, The Book of Kells, and not to forget the center of learning that Irish monasteries had become during Europe's Dark Ages, when, according to my Dad, the English were 'virtually cannibals.'

John Lennon and Paul McCartney's Irish roots could also be thrown in to further tick off the ignorant, pubescent English oafs, he said. Most of the great people in history had been Irish or had Irish roots, he added, including President John F. Kennedy, the man whose portrait was found in nearly every

Irish home, along with Jesus, the Virgin Mary and the Pope.

I eventually won the debate, mainly because my Dad prepped me well. Mention of 'bog people,' us Irish not having cars only donkey-drawn carriages and the shamrock as 'a filthy weed' could not compare to the zingers I hit my opponent with.

"It is undeniable Ireland made a great contribution to world culture," I said, adding as my final parting shot, "And if Ireland was backward in any way, it was only because of England's seven hundred years of misrule."

Such thoughts from years past filtered through my mind now as we followed Dad's funeral hearse along the street.

I noticed a blue-haired punk on a motor-bike who passed by and crossed himself, an act of respect I appreciated. Only then did I fully realise I'd been dealing with the Catholic Church ever since the plane had touched down. I could think all I wanted about Catholicism, but there was no doubt Ireland was united by it. My experience of an English Catholic school full of people who were most definitely not Christian in their behaviour or temperament had left me violently anti-religious. Every ex-Catholic knows the feeling. This mark of respect, however, of common decency, which I noticed almost everyone else doing here in Ireland would be rare in most places, and not just crazy New York.

My reverie was briefly interrupted by our second encounter with the madman from the church the day before. Standing on a street corner raving loudly, he saw the hearse go by and turned his abuse towards it, not knowing it was carrying the very same man he'd already promised to resurrect. We all laughed as we passed him, glad of the light relief.

Springfield Cemetery is located in Bray, just outside Dublin, surrounded by the beautiful Wicklow and Sugarloaf mountains. There were about fifty mourners there when all of a sudden, the warm, balmy weather transformed into a monstrous Irish downpour of dark, miserable sleet. The earth was no longer firm, but muddy and difficult to walk on. An Ireland straight out of the pages of Joyce. The coffin hovered over the grave as priests intoned their prayers. This was the most momentous feeling for me as they prepared to lower my father into the earth. This was the way it was. This is the way it is. This is the way it will be. Now and forever. As the priests continued preaching, I was glad of their litanies.

The rain, the greyness, the coldness. The atmosphere was somehow appropriate as the coffin finally went down below. Mum, who had been calm until this point, began crying, and we all followed. Sons burying a father, a wife burying a husband. It was the second day of the New Year, 1988.

Afterwards, we all went to Mum's house where relatives had prepared sandwiches and drinks. In some ways, I'd been wary of the Irish expression of grief because of the religious sentiments attached, but what I saw happening was quite the reverse. This wasn't morbid at all. I enjoyed what was, in effect, a little party for Dad, a party attended by all my cousins, aunts and uncles, most of whom I hadn't seen in a very long time. I was catching up on all the news, including marriages and babies.

One aunt reminisced about Dad, "Didn't Tony used to write on the back of used sugar bags to his sons when they were at boarding school," she said. " Wasn't he an uninhibited man to do that? Not caring what anybody thought."

What a flashback! How did she know this? I'd totally forgotten about it.

"It wasn't just school, it was college too," I added.

A few days later, a well-meaning priest came to the house. He'd already said several masses for Dad, which we'd attended. Now he wanted to say some more prayers with us, but all we wanted to do was go to the pub, the Killiney Court, overlooking Killiney Bay on one side and Dalkey Island on the another, with the misty Wicklow Mountains in the distance. We wanted to toast our Dad in what was my parents' favorite bar and at the same time enjoy the quiet beauty that is Ireland. The priest had overstayed his welcome, we didn't want to hear or say any more prayers with him, so off we went to the pub.

Dad's tombstone was etched later that year with a quotation from one of his favourite authors, Charles Dickens. The quotation from 'A Tale of Two Cities,' which Dad loved, read: 'It's a far better thing that I've ever done that I do now. It's a far better peace that I've ever known that I go to now. Anthony Mara 1914 –

1987.'

But there was something else on the stone, the name of the stonemasons who'd etched the words. Written in large script, 'The Shanahan Brothers.' Dickens was temporal but the Shanahan Brothers were immortal.

Mum was upset but the rest of us found it funny. Eventually, my brother Dave telephoned the people who we'd quickly dubbed, the 'Shenanigan Brothers.'

"Listen, it's Dave Mara here and the headstone for our Dad is ridiculous," he said. "It looks like a commercial for your company. I don't care if everyone is doing it nowadays. No I didn't look to see if the other stones had adverts on them too. No, Mr. Shanahan, I know cars now have stickers on them advertising where they were bought, but my Dad wasn't a car, okay?"

And so it went on.

Under threat of not being paid the rest of the money owed, the 'Shenanigan Brothers' filled in the offending advertisement. But they must have used a black marker pen to do so because the name eventually came through a year later after a heavy rain, as clear as the day it was etched. My Dad would have laughed about it.

LOVE OVERCOMES ALL

My Mum, Angela Delia Flattery, was born in Salthill, Galway on the west coast of Ireland on August 2, 1918 into a typically large Irish farming family, three girls and six boys, she being somewhere in the middle.

Early in her life, her family was forced to move by a 'Land Commission Relocation' order to Trim in Meath, about 30 miles northwest of Dublin. At that time, Meath land was considered poorer quality than Galway's for farming. However, it was soon discovered that the soil was actually rich and fertile beyond what anybody had previously thought. In other words, 'there was gold in them thar' fields.'

A river, the Blackwater, ran through the Flattery's new farm which was now a larger parcel than the original, perhaps in compensation for the relocation. As such, the farm became prosperous, worked by the boys in the family. Traditionally back then, sons inherited the farm and eventually divided it up, sometimes creating other farms or businesses, which is exactly what the Flatterys did, starting a pub, a grocery and an auction house. The girls received a college education and were expected to marry well. That was how farming dynasties were made then in Ireland.

Accordingly, Mum, who'd developed an interest in chemistry, studied to become a pharmacist. She started her apprenticeship with Hayes, Conyngham and Robinson in Dublin in 1937 when she was nineteen. HCR, as it was known, was a widely-respected pharmacy chain and Mum ended up working for them on and off for the next 50 years, eventually retiring with them.

In those days, being a pharmacist required more skill and knowledge than it does today. It was an exact science, with mortar and pestle in constant use. Pills and capsules were not as omnipresent as they are today. Instead, a pharmacist had to have an encyclopaedic knowledge of what chemical compounds to mix to fill a prescription, and their correct proportions. Medicinal powders were weighed on scales and measured in grams. I know, I saw them doing it.

Only twice in the fifteen years we lived above a chemist's shop in England where my Mum worked did I have to get on my bike to reclaim a prescription that she thought 'wasn't right'. It certainly wasn't a life or death issue, more to do with her being a perfectionist in her profession. On top of this mind-boggling work, doctors' prescriptions were written in Latin. Pharmacists had to understand how to translate these illegibly written doctors' prescriptions into English.

One day, while my Mum was working in the pharmacy, a man walked in, a man whose stature, clothes and hairstyle set him out as an Irish version of Humphrey Bogart. He was Tony Mara, the new pharmacist, his family being Dublin transplants from Newry, Northern Ireland, which they'd left when he was a child. Initially, the Maras moved to Kilkenny before setting up in Dublin. Four years older than Mum, he was a quiet man by nature, certainly compared to Mum who was high-spirited and outgoing and liked to enjoy herself. A country girl by birth, she'd remain one all her life. Dad in contrast was a longtime Dubliner, a man of the city. When they fell for each other in 1940 or 1941, it was a classic meeting of opposites.

But major hurdles faced the new couple when they eventually decided to get married because Mum's family was violently opposed to the union. But come hell or high water, Mum, a determined woman, was going to marry Tony Mara, which, of course, she did. Otherwise, I'd have no story to tell.

Mum's family had met Tony a few times but they hadn't been impressed. For one thing, there had been 'an understanding' that Mum would marry a well-known local farmer in Meath whose nickname was 'The Guzzard' and had a sizeable amount of land, the main reason her parents were opposed to her choice of husband. Dad wasn't even a farmer and therefore didn't have any acreage to bring to the table as a suitor. In rural Ireland of the 1940s that was considered essential. Granddad and Granny weren't happy she wasn't going to marry the farmer. In Ireland then, and probably still now to a lesser extent, land was everything.

Dad said the first time he'd gone to the family farm to meet Mum's parents and brothers, some of whom were still living at home, he'd been politely offered a shot of whiskey by my Granddad. In doing so, my Granddad was courteously showing Dad he was being treated like a man on equal terms and a serious contender for his daughter's hand. As Dad drank whiskey with Granddad, he noticed with some amusement that Granddad's own sons, also young men like him, were given lemonade to drink. Ireland has always been haunted by the curse of 'the Drink' and in his own way Granddad was making sure the lads didn't have any opportunity, at least from him, to be brought down by what was considered a national malaise.

Irish farmers don't deal in abstracts, meaning there's the weather, there's the livestock and there's the land, worked usually by big, muscular people. This was another strike against Dad, for he was small in stature, five-foot-eight on a good day, not a hulking lad like most of the farming Flatterys. He was also considered 'soft'.

Another meeting was set up at a hotel in Dublin to further assess the situation of the two lovebirds, my future parents, who were still determined not to be stopped. My Granddad and brothers assembled to meet Dad at the elegant Shelbourne Hotel on the corner of Kildare Street, its Georgian façade facing St. Stephen's Green. As Mum told me later, Dad was asked by Granddad to come upstairs to a vacant room in a corner of which stood a weighing machine. Much to Dad's surprise, Granddad, a big lad himself, asked Dad to step on the scales, which he dutifully did. I'd imagine he would have come in somewhere around ten and a half stone. What was reported to the brothers waiting downstairs, however, has been left unanswered in my family history.

A lightweight? Soft? My Dad? Not at all, quite the opposite. He had been a member of the Gaelic Athletic Association (GAA), playing hurling, one of two ferocious national sports in Ireland, the other being Gaelic football. Dad played for Kilkenny, a successful national team known as the 'Kilkenny Cats,' with which he won countless trophies. He even played in Croke Park, Dublin – Ireland's prestigious Wembley stadium, and in a final. He had dentures from an early age after his teeth were knocked out during a game. And a broken nose which he never had fixed and that somehow made him look Egyptian as my Mum liked to remark. He had a broken thumb too, also left unfixed, which he could bend backwards to touch his wrist. My Dad might have been a quiet man, but soft? No. He just talked soft, he was tougher than nails. And he carried a big hurley stick around with him. He was a 'Kilkenny Cat' after all.

My parents married on September 14, 1945, a month after World War Two ended, with their reception being held at Dublin's Gresham Hotel. My uncle Ned, my Dad's brother and a newly-ordained priest, officiated. It was a big wedding with everybody from both sides of the family there, with one notable exception, my Grandmother on my Mum's side. She was stubborn, just like my Mum, and while the wedding was accepted begrudgingly by some, my Grandmother was adamant she wouldn't attend.

My Mum wore a dazzling wedding dress. In the black and white photos, it's hard to tell whether it was red or purple. Maybe even scarlet. She looked glamorous, what they called a 'looker' back in the day, more like Rita Hayworth or Ava Gardner than a country girl from Meath getting married in Dublin. Was the dress worn as an act of defiance? Or was it simply a country girl with big ambitions?

LEFT BEHIND

After their marriage, my parents moved to Dean's Grange, a suburb of Dublin, and set up two businesses. First and foremost, a chemist shop. And secondly, a clothing store, both of which they established after borrowing heavily from my Dad's father. They also bought a house.

Armed with their chemistry degrees, they were confident of setting up a niche pharmacy along with the shop. They were taking a big risk. Today Dean's Grange is an exclusive neighbourhood but in the late 1940s and early 1950s it was merely an up-and-coming middle class area, not a certainty for such ambitious enterprises. But my parents prospered reasonably well. They also had a growing family that in seven years would become four boys. When Dave, my eldest brother, was born about a year after their wedding, a rapprochement with my Mum's family was established after a visit to the Flattery farm in

Meath smoothed over lingering opposition to their union.

But another disaster was looming.

In the early 1950s, Granddad Mara died suddenly without leaving a will. Intestate was the technical term, a word I heard constantly growing up. Even though Granny Mara was still alive, in those days Irish society lived by male heirs, not female ones. Other family members now suddenly wanted Dad to pay them back what they felt was their fair share of the money Granddad had loaned him.

Being a scrupulously honest man and disliking family disputes, Dad decided to repay the loan as a matter of honour, even though it meant he and Mum would have to sell their businesses. A religious person, he'd previously spent a year in a seminary, and philosophical by nature, he must have been very disappointed by the actions of certain people, including one of my favourite uncles. A second rapprochement, this time with Dad's family, would have to wait for another day as Mum and Dad sold everything to repay the debt. They also made the fateful decision to move to England where they would become what is now called 'The Forgotten Irish,' meaning 'the invisible generation,' Irish people who moved there in the late 1940s, 1950s and 1960s.

Why England? Despite being only a little more than ten years out of World War Two, England was, and always has been, a reliable source of employment for Irish people. As it's just 'next door,' Irish labourers flocked to it for work. When I worked on construction sites in the mid-1970s, those very same Irish were still there, now middle-aged or older, but still admirably tough.

My parents also made a second fateful decision then - to leave me behind in Ireland.

Two years old, I was the youngest and still not school age, so my parents could not both make a living in England if I stayed. So, when my parents moved to England, I went to live on the Flattery farm in Castlerickard, county Meath, for over two years.

On the farm was my bachelor Uncle Eamon, who would marry much later in life, my Aunt Ev, a spinster, and Granny Flattery. They brought me up for the next couple of years, so I now became a little farm boy as the rest of my family went to live in the shattered England of the mid-1950s.

They had no idea how truly desperate it would be over there for them.

My parents were going to England unusually, as Irish 'middle-class professionals' but with one caveat, which was a thorn in their side the entire time they were there. Their Irish pharmacy degrees weren't recognised and vice-versa for English degrees in Ireland. Technically they couldn't be in charge of English chemist shops and, more importantly, weren't paid the same wages as their fellow qualified English pharmacists. The term for getting equal pay and status was called 'reciprocity,' an agreement between the English and Irish pharmaceutical associations whereby both sides' degrees would be recognised. In those days, human traffic flowed one way as it had for centuries, from Ireland to England, so this lack of reciprocity mainly affected the Irish. A case of ancient politics hurting the innocent. My parents spent twenty years in England and the equality issue was only finalised years after they left.

The first place my parents settled in England was Battersea, south London, then a slum, now a hot real estate area. 1950s London was still devastated from World War Two, destroyed buildings everywhere along with huge bomb craters and air-raid shelters, which I would later play in happily with other children. This was not the Promised Land. England itself was wrecked from coast to coast, not just London. All the major port and industrial cities had been heavily bombed, north to south, east to west. London itself had endured the Nazis blitz and would take decades to rebuild. Not only was Battersea badly bombed, it was also in the path of a vast slum clearance program. Thus, after only a few years, my parents had to vacate their rented home.

As bulldozers demolished buildings behind them on the day they were leaving, guess what they were doing? Tidying up. My eldest brother vividly remembers my parents cleaning the place before they left. Proud as punch, maybe they didn't want English people talking about them behind their backs.

LIFE ON THE FARM

Water lashed over the top of the cast-iron washing machine, splashing down onto the floor, creating a rainstorm on top of the car. I put my hand over the car to protect its occupants. Four miniature policemen, their faces painted flat on to each window. Wearing blue peaked hats, the front two stared blankly ahead. The two in the passenger seats gazed out at me. A battered blue fort stood on the other side of the washing machine. Brightly-colored guards, with flaking paint, stood on the parapet. A new guard, which my uncle had bought me, stood at the fort's entrance.

This is my earliest and most vivid memory at Castlerickard farm in the mid 1950's. My mother had grown up in this house along with six brothers and two sisters. Now I was being raised by her youngest brother Eamon, her sister Evelyn and my Granny, while my parents worked six days a week, sometimes seven, in various chemist shops all over London.

Thus, while the rest of my family was in England, I lived on the farm, initially confused but in the end a happy, spoiled little boy.

There were pigs and sheep on the farm but cows were its mainstay, with herds roaming the fields, the smallest being at the back of the house, home to a dozen or so. I realised that cows despite their huge size, at least relative to me, were the gentlest and friendliest of creatures. I also realised they were intensely curious. They would follow me everywhere. I would often allow several of them to wander behind me through the enclosed field, playing a variation of the same game with them. As they trotted tamely after me, I would pretend I hadn't noticed them. We'd walk together to a gate at the end of the field, then suddenly I would swing round, run at them and disperse them just for fun. At other times, a loud clap would have the same effect. I was already a mighty boy at four years old, scaring livestock.

There were two stately staircases in Castlerickard. One curled its way to the top floor of the house and the adults' bedrooms. The other was a smaller, narrower staircase that led to my bedroom. Every night my Uncle Eamon and I would stand at the bottom of these stairs and race to see who got to my bedroom first. No matter what staircase Uncle Eamon took, he was always in my bedroom before me, laughing. I couldn't work out how he did it. He said there was a secret way which he'd show me when I got older. To this day, I still don't know.

My evenings were sometimes spent by the

fireplace in the living room, holding my arms wide open for my Auntie Ev as she knitted Arran sweaters of varying colors, mainly for me. We'd talk about my day, what I'd done, whom I'd played with. Usually it was was my cousins who were plentiful in town and in the countryside.

Granny would sit there, sometimes listening, sometimes talking, always - like everybody else in the house - drinking lots of cups of tea. She was what they call in Ireland, a 'fierce woman,' with a loud, raspy, often angry voice, which I later found out terrified my cousins but never bothered me because it was never directed at me. I was her boy in Castlerickard and she always looked out for me. So, unlike my trembling cousins, I was very fond of my 'fierce' grandmother.

In many ways, it was an idyllic childhood. Here I was surrounded by cousins who came to play with me most days in my 'castle,' Castlerickard, where I was now king. Being a child, this idyllic childhood seemed to go on forever, until one day, when I was four, a stranger came to take me away to a place called England.

That man was my Dad, a man I barely knew. At least once a year, if not every six months, when he had the money and could get time off work in London, he'd visit, wanting to stay in touch with the son he'd left behind. In those days, a journey from London to Ireland was a full day of crowded trains and ferries, one I would travel too many times when I was older.

Dad was gentle and small compared to my big Meath farmer, Uncle Eamon, whom I looked upon as my real Dad. I was told later that Uncle Eamon and Auntie Ev were very upset and couldn't talk as he took me away to England. Dad also told me that Granny said to him, "He belongs to us, you can't take him. You should never have done this." There were many tears shed in Castlerickard by my aunt, uncle and granny as I left that day. To be honest I don't remember any of that except what happened next, the epic journey to England with my Dad.

WHERE ARE THE COWS?

Dad and I went to the ferry at Dun Laoighaire, near Dublin, and from there sailed to Holyhead in Wales, where trains took us to London. I remember seeing the stars magically bright through the train windows as we moved through the darkness. I'd never experienced an adventure like this before.

We ate supper together, a boiled egg, toast with jam and a cup of tea, the sky outside illuminating us. I'll always remember that meal, the stars looking like those in the great Maurice Sendak story, *In the Night Kitchen*, where Stan Laurel and Oliver Hardy float around like mad chefs with stars shining on their pots and pans. That train journey to England remains firmly fixed in my mind even though my Dad later told me our supper together could never have happened.

"British Rail wouldn't have served boiled eggs or jam with toast for supper back then," he said. "Those trains were essentially cattle cars, bringing us

Irish back and forth to England. And the cattle got treated much better than us."

When we eventually got to the leafy suburb of Mitcham, Surrey about eighteen hours later, I was puzzled by the woman who rushed out to greet me so warmly, a person I simply didn't recognise. It turned out to be my mother.

Inside the house, I met my three brothers, Charlie, Tim and Dave. I didn't remember them either. They were bigger than me. The room we were all sitting in was a disaster. My parents had just bought the house and the previous owners had tried to scrape off all the wallpaper and had also ripped out light fittings in every room. Even as a kid it was a shocking sight.

All I could do was look at my new brothers in this strange room. They told me much later that they had awaited my arrival with great excitement. I was a mystery to them, they thinking 'What will he be like, this little brother of ours from Ireland?' They described me as wearing bright red shoes and suspenders, my hair short and blondish. I also spoke with an Irish accent which they'd already lost.

I recall there was a toy train on the floor with a clockwork key and some tracks beside it. I was told to wind it up and did so, sending it on its way, but didn't put it on the tracks. It ended up smashing into a far wall, making it instantly useless.

To say my siblings were not pleased was a major understatement. 'Who was this strange boy who'd come all the way from Ireland to smash our favorite train?' They tried to rectify the damage, but in vain. As it was an accident, I fervently I hoped my brothers wouldn't hate me.

Later, we all went up to Mitcham Common, a vast green open space like Castlerickard, but very different. Men here played soccer on every rectangular field available. I later learned the teams consisted mainly of Polish air-pilots and other army personnel who had come over to fight in the war. They'd stayed in England for the same reasons as my parents, for work, but also to escape their newly Soviet Communist controlled country. I ended up going to school with their children and becoming good friends.

As I gazed at the mowed fields all around me and all the activity going on, I suddenly turned to my Dad, "Where are my Uncle Eamon, Auntie Ev and Granny?" Silence ensued as he considered his response, later telling me he was even less prepared for my next question. "And where are all the cows?"

PEEING IN THE FOUNTAIN

Even though I would not be five for another six months, therefore technically not eligible for primary school, my parents somehow finagled me in. After all, that was the main reason they'd brought me to England.

There were three Mara boys there already, and it seemed only right I should join them, too young or not. So come Monday, the weekend after first arriving in England, I turned up at St. Peter and Paul's Primary School with my brothers to be shown around.

I was an instant sensation. Some older girls were put in charge of me and they literally picked me up to display me to their pals as if I was a cuddly teddy bear. I had been truly adopted and, with my blond hair, I was paraded around the school as a cutesy package.

My Irish accent also wowed them.

"Isn't he gorgeous? Say something Joseph," they'd say to me.

This carried on throughout my first morning at school and then something happened that would later become a much-quoted incident in family folklore.

Near a water fountain in the schoolyard I asked the girls to let me down. They watched me as I toddled towards the fountain to do what they assumed any normal person would do - have a drink. Not me. I was overcome by a much more primal urge. Undoing my fly, I happily urinated straight into the fountain. I was a farm boy from Castlerickard after all and I was used to taking a pee wherever and whenever I wanted. The girls abandoned me instantly in horror. I'd suddenly gone from adorable to vile. The head girl told me while I could do that In Ireland, I couldn't do it in England.

Tim would relate this story endlessly through the ensuing decades, much to my mother's horror and my undying embarrassment. Told in an Irish accent, he'd say, "And so wasn't Joe like a 'baste' of the field. He saw a fountain and mistook it for a water spot for cows on the farm. So, he walked over to it and naturally did what he was used to doing like the bastes of the field back home. But this was too much for the English schoolgirls who were outraged by this appalling little Irish boy's action. Why, they'd carried him around all day as this adorable little feller with the cute blonde curls and now he'd done something utterly disgusting."

My mother would protest, "Will you stop Tim

with this horrible story? Haven't we heard it enough times already?" Yes, we most definitely had, and I was usually squirming and blushing in my seat even into my early 40s upon hearing it yet again.

After leaving the bombed-out slum of Battersea, my parents bought a house in suburban Mitcham. Big enough for a family of six, it had a large garden that we four boys played together in. So now we were living in a leafy suburb of London instead of the south London dump of Battersea, a place I'd never truly experienced because I'd been most of the time at Castlerickard.

Like most kids, I quickly adapted to my new home, complete with 'new brothers' and 'new parents'. Next door to us lived an Indian family called the Browns and on the other side was a Nigerian couple, the Wallaces. In Ireland there were no people of colour in those days. I'd never actually seen a 'coloured person' before. But my parents and the Indian and Nigerian families were in the same boat, immigrant families trying to make their way in the new harsh land of war-ravaged England. But as kids, we didn't much care. For us, the bomb-shelters were simply fun places to play in and we'd play with anyone who wanted to, regardless of colour.

We four 'wild colonial boys' would fashion rudimentary yet potentially lethal weapons from wood we'd found on Mitcham Common at the end of our street and we'd 'stage' ferocious battles with homemade swords in the garden. Observers might think we were trying to knock each other's heads off but in fact we staged our fights so kind Mrs. Wallace would rush out bearing one of her luscious homemade apple, pear or peach pies as a bribe for us to stop. She won us over every time, of course.

Being at work, my parents weren't around for a few hours after school so Mrs. Wallace became our de facto babysitter. Her husband wore well-pressed suits to work and was away a lot and I was told later he had a 'good job.' Both the Wallaces and the Browns were great neighbours.

The Browns also had a pretty daughter called Jennifer, roughly my age, who'd often play with us. I soon became smitten, hoping one day when I was older we'd get married. Where are you now Jennifer Brown? More than 50 years later, I still dream of you, waiting for you at the bottom of the garden.

Meanwhile, we were introduced to Mrs. Brown's curries, an exotic food unheard of in Ireland. If Mum or Dad was home doing some chore inside the house, Mrs. Brown or Mrs. Wallace would keep an eye on us in the garden over the fence. I soon settled into life in Mitcham, finding new friends during my very first day of school, the 'water fountain incident' already a distant memory. A big school, I still have fond memories of it to this day. It faced on to Cricketers' Green, an open grassland where we played a zany style of football, 40 energy-charged kids chasing a single ball as if it was a writhing snake.

I was truly one of the brothers now and in a year or two I would forgo getting a bus with Charlie who was initially in charge of me and run the mile home through Mitcham Common to our house at Dahlia Gardens. The world was a less dangerous place then, no worries about kids going back and forth to school. The Common itself was expansive, containing the Three Kings Ponds and the Seven Islands Ponds, that seemed like lakes to us, all bordered by hills and lots of bushes and tall trees.

Our parents worked Saturdays as did all chemists, so they had to come up with some way to keep us busy and out of trouble that day. That's how it became 'cinema day.' I'd join my brothers at the 'ABC Minors Club' in nearby Thornton Heat where we'd watch films and serials from morning to early afternoon with hundreds of other kids. Here prizes were given out if you sat absolutely still when the appropriate music came on to warn you the usher's torch might spotlight you. Hundreds of boisterous kids would suddenly freeze en masse. It was a great idea and it worked. To further encourage good behavior, ABC Minor Club badges were given out so you could show your parents you'd been well-behaved. It was a great system which kept thousands of kids calm in the darkness of cinemas all over England in the late 1950s and early 1960s.

Of course, we all loved 'the pictures.'

I still remember seeing the haunting 'Whistle Down the Wind' at the ABC for the first time. Like every other kid in the cinema, I truly believed escaped convict, Alan Bates, who told farm kids who found him hiding in a barn, that he was Jesus. I imagined smuggling food to him in the barn along with the beautiful Hayley Mills and her friends, while grown-ups searched for him.

Then there was the Westerns that ended with the heroes riding off into a glorious sunset, then immediately returning to begin the exact same film all over again. Once more they came riding through the glorious dawn exactly as they had done when the film first started. There was no break in the film and I thought it would never end but of course this was an impossible dream, a child's creation. I still enjoy replaying it in my mind even now as if it was reality - *'the never-ending film.'* It was like my train-dinner-with-my-Dad memory, which still remains so vivid to me. To this day, I still think my recollection of that trip was right and my Dad's was wrong.

Within a year of arriving in England, I'd lost my Irish accent, much to the dismay of my Uncle Eamon, Auntie Ev and Granny when I returned to visit them for the first time.

"Joseph, what happened to your accent? How did you lose it?" they asked, shocked.

CONDOMS, THE PILL AND JUNKIES

My parents faced many challenges as chemists but one of the most peculiar was one that collided with their Catholic Irish upbringing.

In a word, condoms.

'Chemical indignities' to some and Durex or 'rubbers' to others. Names that induced millions of teenage to snigger since they were first introduced in England.

Being from a country that didn't allow divorce, let alone contraceptives, my parents, like all Irish chemists, needed special dispensation from the Pope to provide such things to the people of this 'pagan' country. I remember Dad telling us about how he was once asked for 'rubber goods' by a young customer and innocently replied, "What size would you like?" as he rummaged in a drawer for rubber gloves.

In the early and mid-60s, an even greater challenge faced by parents - 'the Pill.' That involved prescriptions, not simple over-the-counter stuff, and Mum, albeit disapprovingly, provided it to 'mini-skirted dolly birds' as they were known then. A sexual revolution was underway in the '60s and my strict Irish parents felt they were providing 'weapons' for it. Dad faced an even more challenging situation than Mum because of a second job he had at Boots Chemists, Piccadilly in central London where 'rubbers' were in strong demand.

So hard-working was Dad, he didn't usually arrive home until after midnight, so we'd rarely see him. Somehow, however, he always managed to bring me a plastic dinosaur model to add to my carefully-arranged collection on my bedroom mantelpiece. I thought it had appeared by magic. I'd wake up next day and there it was - a colourful creature that had mysteriously appeared out of the night from mythical Piccadilly Circus.

Much later, when I was about twelve, I was given a dramatic insight into my father's work. In what I now consider was his way of teaching me a lesson about life, he brought me to Piccadilly and we had lunch at the nearby Lyons Corner House. Suddenly, he started buying cups of tea for a couple of people who were behaving strangely. One, a girl of about 19, was nodding off into her teacup and had appalling sores on her face and hands. When I asked, Dad told me she was a drug addict and that he served heroin to her, and others like her, at Boots. Liberalism in mid-60s England meant small doses of heroin were legally prescribed to drug-addicts. The sores the girl suffered from were a side-effect of the barbiturates she had been prescribed to help get her off heroin.

After that, my Dad took me to a 'junkie haven' on the steps of the Eros statue in Piccadilly where addicts waited to get their prescriptions from Boots, directly opposite, the only place in London where people could get medicine late at night. These were early hard core addicts who'd suddenly appeared in all the major cities, especially London. It was a new and ugly phenomenon and the harbinger of things to come. Boots in Piccadilly had become the epicentre of this attempt to wean addicts off heroin. Dad was sympathetic to these hopeless young junkies, mere boys and girls, but he simply couldn't understand it. It seemed to him his adopted country was getting out of control.

ON THE MOVE AGAIN

When I was nine, my parents made another momentous decision.

They sold our Mitcham house and rented a two-floor apartment above a chemist's shop in an even more leafy suburb of London called Ashtead in Surrey.

This meant Mum could work in the shop below while Dad commuted to London. As for the money from the house sale, it was used to pay for our education in the best Catholic School in south (or 'sarf') London, St. Joseph's School, known for its academic prowess.

Mum, the main family decision-maker, thought we should do the best we could in this new land because she'd determined we were going to be here for a while. I realised later that Dad had a somewhat different reason for wanting us to go to St. Joseph's - a decidedly Catholic education. The school was administered by the De La Salle brothers, originally a

French order that migrated to England. They wore long black robes and white mitres, evoking images of the Christian Brothers back home who had taught Dad.

Years later, as an adult, I understood his reasoning. He was religious and didn't want our Irish Catholic background undermined by Protestant England. Back then, to be Irish was to be Catholic, to be Catholic was to be Irish. It was all bound together in Ireland. In largely secular, foreign England it just didn't matter. But for the Irish this had been their core for centuries, their national identity, to preserve their culture against cruel invaders, the English. So now we too had to maintain our identity in this so-called 'heathen' country.

Priests visited us regularly in Mitcham, some of whom Mum and Dad knew from back home in Ireland, or at least knew their kinfolk. Some of them liked a 'drop' of whiskey and some of them liked more than a drop and subsequently talked a lot to my parents and us. Even as a kid I remember a few of them being what I'd now call obsequious and quite drunk sometimes. But they knew they had the newly-arrived Irish in England by the short and curlies. We were their subjects in this new land.

Often we'd have to kneel with them beside sofas or chairs in the living room and pray. Dad, who was more religious than Mum, made sure we all said the Rosary every night. We'd say ten Hail Marys, one Our Father and a prayer involving the, 'vale of tears and gnashing of teeth.' I remember thinking this sounded like the worst place ever, one I definitely didn't want to go to. If this continued, we were truly going to remain both Irish and Catholic in this so-called heathen country.

Three of my brothers were boarders at St. Joseph's but being the youngest, or simply because they couldn't afford it, I was kept at home twenty miles away, travelling to school every day.

I loved Mitcham, we all did. So the news we were leaving came as a shock. We had wonderful neighbours who put up with us noisy boys. Our parents, especially my mother, instilled in us politeness to a fault so one warning over the fence was enough for us to stop any over-the-top hi-jinks. An Indian accent saying, "Are you not having enough space up on the big common?" stopped us dead in our tracks.

We were never rude to grown-ups, we were told they were to be treated with respect. For instance, we always stood up out of our seats when adults entered the room. To this day, even in pubs, I'll rise and shake an acquaintance's hand if they come over to talk to me.

"No, no, you don't have to get up…"

"Oh, yes I do."

St. Peter and Paul's and Mitcham were great places to be and our friends were many. Sometimes in the evenings we'd even play football with Dad on the big common at the top of the street. He was still fairly fit in his late 40s, being strong and athletic from his hurling and Gaelic footballing days. And a mighty swimmer, as evidenced when we went to the local pool with him. He also loved to walk long distances and later I'd often join him in on Ashtead Common. That's probably why he stayed the same weight and height from his '20s to the very end.

Perhaps the reason I found it especially difficult to leave Mitcham was because it reminded me of having to leave Castlerickard. That's probably why I did something that, not for the first time, landed me in trouble.

I wrote a letter shortly after we arrived in Ashtead to Bernie Rayner, my best friend at St. Peter and Paul's, telling him I hated Ashtead and was going to leave and come back to Mitcham and live there instead. Maybe, I thought, I could live at his house as the Rayners, also of Irish descent, would surely take me in. Wise Bernie, all of nine years old, showed the letter to his parents who immediately mailed it to mine, warning them of my impending departure. I don't remember being heavily chastised but if it's possible for a child to suffer embarrassment I certainly did when I saw my returned letter. I was told I'd get used to the school, that yes, it was a little different from St. Peter and Paul's, but over time it would get better. And it did.

To this day, I still proudly have a photograph of the St. Peter's team I played on that won the all-Surrey Football Championship title in 1964. The final was on an unusually hot day in England, a fantastic game from start to finish. Peter Benson, a winger, was a standout player for us, scoring the winning goal in the last minute of the game. Even joyous adults told us we came from behind to win just like grown-up footballers in a real FA Cup final. Years later, I tracked Peter through an obscure site for Ashtead and emailed him, telling him he had been the star player in that game, a true legend.

Peter had moved to America years before me, to California, then New York and eventually settled in Nashville with his family. Mentioning the heroic game we'd played, I asked what his memories were of it. While I still had the child's heroic vision of him in my memory, he couldn't remember it at all when I told him we'd won the trophy. I even had a picture of it and sent it to him. But even after seeing it, he still had no memory of the event, which admittedly had taken place some 50-odd years before. But there he was in the picture with the other kids, some of whom he recognised.

The game also signalled the end of my last year at St. Peter's. I was headed to St. Joe's in Upper Norwood, south London, where two of my brothers already studied. Dave, my eldest brother, was at Holy Family, Morden, in Surrey but he greeted me at St. Joe's as he transferred there for his final year.

In the end, my parents were right about St. Peter's. Stodgy conservative Ashtead was equal to Mitcham, in a different way. As I prepared to enter St. Joe's, my eleven-year-old life had improved tremendously.

Early on, one of my pals from Ashtead came up to my school and remarked upon seeing the clerics,

"Who's that bloke in a skirt?"

As a teenager 'sarf' London became my stomping ground and Crystal Palace my de facto football team. I also enjoyed the pub scene. Though the legal age for drinking alcohol was eighteen, I was a tall 16-year-old and usually faced no problems getting drinks for myself and my mates.

LIFE-CHANGING EXAM

In England, before going to secondary school, equivalent to high school in America, pupils had to sit what I term 'an insidious exam' known as the 11-Plus, one that could easily shape the rest of your life.

To understand the context, it's best to understand that the England I grew up in was a hierarchical society, with class more important than race. Though it's less like that now, class still exists in certain enclaves, which is why at the time of writing this memoir, two out of the last three English Prime Ministers were educated at Eton, the most elite, expensive, private school in the country.

For the rest of us, the working and middle classes, passing the 11-Plus meant a free scholarship at a 'good' grammar school like St. Joseph's and failure meant attending 'a secondary modern' vocational school where students learned a trade and usually received lower-quality education.

This proved true for my eldest brother Dave

who'd failed the 11-Plus less than a year after he arrived in England at age ten. He used to joke that he only failed because he spoke Gaelic at the time. Dave ended up at a secondary modern school called Holy Family in Morden, Surrey for a year before he went to St. Josephs. Holy Family was a Catholic school but in name only because, alas for Dave, it unfortunately lived up to the general reputation of secondary moderns. It was so rough that rowdy kids sometimes threw compasses at teachers when they were bored or angry. My parents got Dave out of there as soon as they could afford it.

Next up for the 11-Plus was Tim, who aced the exam, as he would do with most things in life, thus earning himself a free scholarship to St. Joseph's. Even though Charlie failed, he still went to St. Joseph's as a boarder. My turn for the 11-Plus came at St. Peters in Ashtead, with my parents promising me a new bike if I passed. Surprisingly, I was invited for 'a special interview.'

I, one other boy and two girls, were interviewed separately for at least forty-five minutes by a smiling lady and a gruff, rather unfriendly, dark-suited man. The lady offered me a sweet but, having been warned not to accept sweets from strangers, I politely declined.

Meanwhile, the man tried to trip me up with a rapid series of mathematic problems. After that, I had to read a passage from a book I was given. When I finished that I then had to answer multiple questions. Only then was the 'interview' over.

My parents and I waited nervously for the results. Even at that young age I knew how much this meant to them. Plus, I still wanted that bike. The day finally came. Our young lay teacher came into class and with tears in her eyes informed the four of us that we had failed the interview. We cried, as did other kids who were our friends.

Crushed, I now faced the onerous task of informing my parents. No school telephone call, no letter in the mail, just me, at eleven years old, telling my parents the bad news.

I arrived home still half-expecting my new bicycle to be there because I'd studied so hard. It must have been a bad blow for my parents for now they had two fee-paying kids at school and they were already arguing about bills which I didn't remember them ever doing.

Dad shook his head, telling me, "I thought you could have done better than that, Joe." It was the first time I ever remembered being disappointed in him.

Luckily for me, however, but not for Charlie who'd already left school to pursue a career in banking, Surrey Council decided to launch a new exam two years later called the 13-Plus. This time I made no mistake, ensuring I would be a non-fee paying St. Joseph's boy for at least five years, until I was eighteen. Believe it or not, I still expected to be given the newest version of the bike I'd been promised, but it didn't materialise.

So now, in 1964, here I was at St. Joseph's School, Beulah Hill, London, a change from the previous two schools with St. Peter in their names. On the first day, I was hit so hard by my new teacher, Mr. Walsh, a red imprint of his hand remained on my face for hours. Hardly the most encouraging start to a hopeful academic career.

HEY BRO, IT'S THE '60S

It was 1968, I was a young teenager and I was the classic 'rebel without a cause.'

That is, until the hippies' era came along. Everybody older than me was having so much fun, but I was only 15. And I was at a school I hated. To me, the De La Salle brothers in their long black robes and white collars who taught me in south London, were caught in a time warp, stranded in the 18th century. Outside the school's high walls were the *'Swinging '60s'* but inside, *'discipline' took the place of 'freedom.'*

For example, there were regular haircut inspections and if your hair overlapped your jacket collar, you faced detention and were forced to cut it that same day or endure a caning. Clothes defined as 'youth culture,' such as mod 'shortie terylene raincoats' that stretched halfway to your knee like a mini-skirt, were banned. Flimsy and useless against harsh English winters, yes, but they were oh, so stylish. Also banned were 'Cuban heels' worn by the Beatles and the Rolling Stones.

Punishment for flaunting school rules was severe. I remember a quiet boy being caned publicly and viciously on the rostrum for wearing 'youth culture' clothes at one of our morning assemblies. The caner, ironically called Brother Solomon, the 'Prefect of Discipline,' seemed to take sadistic pleasure in beating the living daylights out of him.

By the end of 1969 my relationship with my parents had also become fraught. Being Irish in England, they were much stricter than my English friends' parents. I even had to be home earlier than everyone else every night.

Rebellion was therefore inevitable and natural, both on the school front and the home one too. I started missing curfews, I grew my hair longer, I wore 'forbidden' clothes at school. And I really couldn't care less.

As cruel Brother Solomon had been banished after disgracing himself on a school trip to France by using the word 'merde' on a radio show when he was drunk, in reference to our headmaster, I felt it time to 'storm the walls' and see what happened.

I was now the proud possessor of the widest pair of flared trousers in the school and instead of standard black shoes I proudly and defiantly sported a pair of what I thought were very fetching green ones. Brother Paul, who'd taken over as second-in-command from the vanquished Solomon, was more of a progressive liberal, so instead of publicly caning me or expelling me (which he eventually did anyway), he'd ask me what my green shoes 'said' to me. To be honest, I felt like replying with an obscenity but just responded with a fey hippie remark, or the occasional sarcasm, "I just wanna' be free, man."

Finally, Brother Paul called my parents for a meeting to discuss my general attitude and clothing choices. When my Mum returned home, she was furious, mainly because I'd said the reason I wore green shoes to school was because my parents couldn't afford black ones.

In the end, it was rugby that saved me.

The school headmaster, Brother Leo, was the team coach and liked me because I was good at the sport, especially at drop kicks. His view was that he was more interested in what went on in my head than what I wore on my feet. And it was he who came up with a creative solution to the shoe dilemma. With three boys to raise and various school costs to pay, my parents were virtually broke so simply buying a new pair of shoes wasn't that easy.

"I have a compromise," Brother Leo said to me one day. "Why not dye your green shoes black?"

To tell the truth I was pretty sick of the green shoes by then so I took them to a cobbler and for very little money he dyed them perfectly.

That gave me another idea to help boost my growing reputation at school. Much to his astonishment, I'd been wearing some of Dad's old jackets. They were double-breasted, had wide lapels and were very much back in fashion. But I had also noticed my brother Dave's green overcoat hanging in an upstairs cupboard, left there from his days in the Territorial Army. It had super wide lapels, was triple double-breasted and ultra-long too, almost calf length. Very much the style back then. What if I dyed it dark blue, I thought, just like the military overcoats the hippies wore? All I had to do was do it right. So I did it myself.

This involved careful dyeing followed by placing it for a night in a bath-tub of cold water to get rid of residue, hanging it on a washing line for a day or two to dry it, then a trip to the dry cleaners to literally seal the deal. It looked great when I picked it up a week later. I was all set for my proud appearance in school.

Much to my surprise, the coat was not on the banned list, so wearing it I felt 'real cool.' In other words, 'it was quite the dog's bollocks.' Of course, I made no mention of the coat's humble origins, its age or the horribly un-cool green military colour it had been. Aside from its clear fashion statement, it was also very practical, keeping me warm during those damp English winters.

Dare I say it, but the coat made me look like a million dollars. That is until the night Mum got mad at me for missing one curfew too many. In her anger, she threw a bag of flour at me which, though it missed me, exploded all over my cool coat. I rushed out of the house cursing to high heaven, and went to see my hippie mates in the park up the street. One of them looked at me in amazement, then shouted, "Flour Power."

SOUL KITCHEN

Though we liked to call our place in the park our 'Soul Kitchen' after Jim Morrison's famous song, it was hardly that. More a pavilion where 20 or so of my friends hung out. But in the singer's immortal words, it was, 'Still one place to go.'

There, we'd do what most teenagers do: smoke, drink, and hook up with girls. The latter usually didn't pan out as Dads in Ashtead sensibly protected their daughters from 'ne'er-do-wells' like us.

On that particular 'flour power' night, I decided to stay out as long as I wanted. I was already in trouble so what did it matter. I'd go home at 5 or 6. What was PC Plod, our only policeman, going to do? Bother us in the park on a Saturday night? Hardly. He was probably well tucked-up in bed himself.

I should mention that in those days I had two very different sets of friends – those in suburban Ashtead and those at my school. Living in Ashtead's only council estate, equivalent to what are called 'the projects' in America, the former did a few more drugs and indulged in a little more carnal pleasure than my school-friends. They were 'rougher around the edges' and got up to more mischief.

Take for example, the miniature golf escapade. Some of the lads broke into the park ranger's hut one night, took out all the golf clubs and balls and proceeded to have a drunken contest at three in the morning. There was too much of the Irish altar boy in me so usually I wasn't involved in such capers, often going instead to the pub with Dad for a few pints after Sunday church and chatting with his old biddy friends. Each time, it seemed Dad would utter the same line, "Ah boys, somewhere underneath this mass of hair is my son. Speak up Joseph so they know it's you." It was like a scene out of the BBC series, 'Last of the Summer Wine' about a few old men getting together.

Sadly, hard drugs came to Ashtead, in the form of acid and speed, and I witnessed some of my closest friends getting stoned every day.

After forty years or so, I got in touch with someone from those bygone 'Soul Kitchen' days. I was curious to find out if my three closest friends back then were okay and had done well in life. But, alas, Mick Budd, with whom I'd played the greatest football match of my life to win the All-Surrey Football Trophy, had died in his 20s from a drug overdose. Martin Lightfoot, a lovable rogue, had lasted until his 40s, dying also from long-term drug abuse. And, lastly, gentle Roy Jordan, who had departed this earth ten years before, from the same malaise.

BATTLE OVER THE BOOK

Even though Dad was a well-read, well-educated man, there was a side to him that was attracted to some of the more 'colourful' aspects of popular culture.

Boxing, for example. There was nothing he liked more on a Saturday afternoon than watching a good punch-up on television, even if it was between opposing rugby players. The nastier, the better. He found it all so amusing.

He also liked pulp fiction such as *'The Carpetbaggers'* by Harold Robbins. One book he read was called *'What Makes Sammy Run?'* by Budd Schulberg, similar in style to Robbins' racy novels featuring sensuous women with heaving bosoms. I was warned severely not to read this particular book but, of course, that meant I wanted to read it even more. After all, who could resist a book cover featuring mysterious women with low-cut dresses?

I knew where Dad kept the book and while he

was at work I'd take it down to the shed at the end of our garden to read it. Half the mystery was the Sammy character. Who was he? I knew only one Sammy and that was Sammy Davis, Jr. so I assumed the book was about him, but it wasn't. There were big-breasted, heavy-breathing women everywhere as Sammy moved through Hollywood. But I still couldn't understand what all the fuss was about, why I was banned from reading it.

One day Dad arrived home unexpectedly early from work and looked around for his book. Unable to find it, he asked if I knew where it was. I had no choice but to own up.

"It's in the shed, I've been reading it," I said apologetically.

He hit me instantly. A hard slap to my cheek the likes of which I'd not experienced before.

"I told you not to read it," he said.

Dad had never hit any of us before, unlike Mum who hit us with anything from a wooden spoon to her bare hands, and we expected that. To our minds, it was County Meath style justice. As far as we knew, all Irish mothers hit their children like that. But Dad? The quiet man?

As I recall, I stood there shocked and probably tearful. Realising what he'd done, Dad went out of his way over the following days to strengthen the bond between us, for even to him it was a shocking incident. It wasn't long before we were back on track.

OFF TO COLLEGE

Keen to get away from prissy southern England and experience the north's legendary grittiness and down-to-earth sensibilities, I chose to attend Hull Art College, 200 miles northeast of London.

Two years before, I'd gone to Farnham Art College, twenty miles south of Ashtead. Farnham was richer and even more conservative than Ashtead but I sensed Hull would be a very different place. I relished the thought of the adventures I was going to have.

I'd never been up north before until my interview there and I'd been impressed. Demolished and abandoned houses abounded, reminding me of pictures I'd seen in England of the South Bronx. It was even rougher looking than I'd imagined. I was ready for a new start.

I loved the four years I spent there and saw a good part of the region too, getting a better understanding of England in the process. For all its' hick qualities, Hull had a vibrant student exchange program with New York's Fredonia College and while I didn't get to go, I did make strong connections with the incoming American students. They turned out to be fateful meetings for four years after leaving Hull I myself ended up emigrating to America and never returning to live in Europe again.

STRANGE INCIDENT AT A TRAIN STATION

So there I was one afternoon in early March, 1974, a twenty-year-old student at Hull Art College waiting for a train to take me to my parents' home in Ashtead.

I was at Epsom station one stop from Ashtead and could take whatever train came from Ewell West or Ewell East on adjacent platforms, one in front of me, the other behind.

When both trains came along, however, I took neither. Nor did I take the train after that. Why? Well, being an inveterate newspaper reader, I wanted to finish an interesting article I'd started and didn't mind if it took me a little longer getting home.

At the time, I was staying temporarily with my parents as I was on what's called a 'gap year' when students take time off from college to experience the real world. Except my gap year had turned to two and

I had moved all over the country doing all sorts of odd jobs in places like Cornwall and Devon in the west, Kent on the east coast, Hastings in the south, as well as a stint in London. The work varied, from construction jobs, including renovating old houses and erecting scaffolding for a travelling funfair, to potato and hop picking in Kent, the most back-breaking work I'd ever done. The reason I was at Epsom train station was that my last job was working on a survey for Surrey County Council there.

As I sat on a bench reading, I suddenly became aware of two people, a man and a woman, circling me, watching me warily. The man, stout with balding hair, was probably in his mid-forties and wore a tatty blue suit. The woman was in her mid-thirties with dyed blonde hair. She wore an out-of-fashion mini-skirt and black boots that stretched to her knees. As they continued stalking me, I wondered if they were day-release patients from one of the nearby so-called 'mental homes,' where I had once worked as a porter.

"Funny that," the man said suddenly.

"What's funny?" I replied, surprised.

"You didn't take any of the last three trains that came here."

"So what?"

"It's peculiar." Then he hesitated, "Where do you live?"

"Ashtead, if it's any of your business."

"It is my business. You could have taken any train you wanted yet you chose to stay here."

I rustled my newspaper angrily. "Yeah, I'm

reading if it's alright with you."

The man and the woman stood directly in front of me. "Where were you on February 12th?" the man asked.

"I don't know," I snapped back. "Was I with you? If I'm being honest, I don't remember you at all. Doesn't seem like we'd go to the same parties."

His tone changed immediately. "Look sonny, I don't like smart arses, okay? Carry on like that and you'll be in the nick."

Just then, he and the blonde woman produced badges indicating they were detectives. Suddenly, they'd gotten my attention.

"We're investigating a serious crime, so if you don't mind we'd like to talk to you. Either at the police station if you want to be a smart arse. Or at our office here on the platform." Thinking I'd better co-operate we walked to a small room nearby.

Mr. Blue, as I nicknamed him, began his questioning. "Where were you on February 12 then?"

"No idea except I was living in Cornwall."

"Can you verify that? Any witnesses?"

I pretended to look over my shoulder looking for them. "No, not at the moment." "Being a smart arse again are we?" he said. "You'd better stop that, I'm warning you. We're investigating the brutal rape of an elderly woman who was almost beaten to death in a train compartment between here and Ashtead. She's still in a coma. Still think this a joke, son?"

My expression probably indicated I didn't.

"We want to show you a picture of the victim. See if it jogs your memory. You okay with that?"

"Why would it jog any memory? It's got nothing to do with me."

"If that's true, then you won't mind looking at the picture will you?"

"I don't want to see it."

"Why not?"

"I just don't want to see it, alright."

In the movies, when a suspect doesn't want to look at a crime scene, it proves he's got something to hide. He probably can't take it because he'll give himself away with a panic-stricken look, or an odd reaction. But that wasn't my reason. I simply didn't want to look at a photo. Because of my long hair, I'd been often stopped and questioned by police, sometimes searched for drugs, but I'd never been involved in anything bad.

Ignoring my protest, the man shoved the photo across the table.

"Look at it," he barked.

"No."

"Alright, time to go to the station then son"

While I was rebellious, I wasn't stupid. One never knew what cops could do to you at the station, you could get beaten up until you confessed or just held overnight or longer on suspicion. Some of my friends had experienced this and I didn't want it happening to me. I had a look.

The photo was worse than I thought it would be. The unfortunate woman had suffered appalling injuries. Her nose was severely broken, both eyes blackened, her mouth was bloody and there was extensive bruising around her neck as if somebody had tried to strangle her. She was in her early 70s but it was hard to tell due to the state she was in. She was lying against a carriage door unconscious, unknowingly being documented by a police photographer, I assumed. It was a horrendous picture, one I'll never forget.

"Anything to say son?"

"No, I know nothing about this, it's terrible," I said, handing the picture back.

"I've got another I'd like to show you." I didn't protest. "It's a picture of the suspect our police artist produced."

Blue handed me what looked like a facsimile of an artist's pencil drawing. It shocked me, for it looked like me. A scruffy-looking post hippie sort of a man with unkempt hair and a beard.

"What do you think?" Blue asked, almost smiling triumphantly.

"Well, I do admit there's a similarity but this could also be Abraham Lincoln."

I was back in cheeky mode. "Tell you what, why don't you go down to Epsom Art College, you'll find dozens of people looking like this."

His smile faded.

What I had said was true. Everybody was in their post-hippie phase, the scruffy look was cool.

"Empty your pockets," Blue suddenly shouted. "Now."

I took out the only two things I had. My Post Office book and another small book in which I wrote my daily dreams.

"What's this, then?" Blue asked, holding the latter.

"A dream book."

"A dream book, eh? That's a bit peculiar, isn't it?"

He turned to Blondie beside him for support but she remained silent.

"Well, Freud wrote his dreams down," I replied.

"Who?"

"You know, the famous psychoanalyst."

"I know who he is, sonny, I'm just wondering how someone like you would come up with the same idea."

Later, my older brother Tim, upon hearing about the train incident, imitated Blue as if he was a fictional stereotype of a non-too-smart English policeman back in the day. "So, son are you and this Frood accomplices in this 'orrible crime you've committed?"

Meanwhile, Blondie was looking at me a little kindly. Was she playing good cop to his bad?

Then suddenly I realised I might have the upper hand. "Look at this officer."

"I'm not an officer, I'm a detective."

"Okay de-tec-tive, see this?'

"See what?"

I waved my Post Office Savings book at him. "I

have an entry in it for February 12 and guess what. It's postmarked Penzance Post Office, in Cornwall."

"That doesn't prove anything, you could easily have committed this crime and gone back to Cornwall."

"What am I? Some sort of criminal mastermind? Two hundred and fifty odd miles away, five hours by British Rail? Who are you kidding? What time did the crime take place anyway?"

I realised Blue had no interest in telling me because it would clear me, he was more interested in my dream book. It was then the thought crossed my mind they might try to 'stitch me up.' I began to feel uneasy. The Metropolitan Police in London had already been involved in a big corruption scandal along with their elite colleagues, 'The Flying Squad,' in which innocent people were framed.

Blue continued reading my dream book. "Who's this girl sitting on your private parts here, then?"

"I can't help my dreams, they're involuntary," I said. "Haven't you ever had erotic dreams, detective?"

"No, never," came his retort. "Nothing like this filth anyway."

There were plenty of other dreams in the book that weren't sexual but he ignored them. Then suddenly he said, "You know what? You want to get out of this right now, right?"

I nodded.

"Why don't we give you a lift home, have a

quick look over your place and make sure everything's okay. Alright? If it is, we'll be out of your hair, son. You'd like that, right?"

Just to get them off my back, I agreed, so we left Epsom Railway station. As we made our way to my home, the local girl's school, Rosewood, was emptying for the day. We stopped at a pedestrian crossing to let some students go by. It was then I recognised someone, Carole, who'd been my girlfriend on and off for years. If I could show her off to Blue and Blondie, it might end their suspicions that I was some sort of serial rapist. I called her over and she gazed at the two people in the car quizzically.

"Hi Carole, these two people are police officers who believe I've been involved in a rape," I said deadpan.

She laughed, "Are you serious? You?"

"Yep. They're taking me home to search my place and then we're done. Officers er - detectives - can we give Carole a lift home, she lives near me."

Blue wasn't happy, replying curtly, "No. We're not a taxi service."

I shrugged and Carole turned to go, saying "Good luck" as she walked away.

"So who's she then?" Blue asked.

"An old girlfriend."

"Why'd you break up?"

"Oh, the usual reasons detective, you know."

"No, I don't know."

"Well, I've been away a lot so we drifted apart. But we're still good friends."

My house was on top of a chemist shop where Mum worked. To get in, you had to go round the back, through the garden and up some ugly black iron stairs to our door. Blue, Blondie and I went up, but when we got to the top, the door was already open. Seeing the three of us standing there, Mum looked puzzled.

Knowing how volatile and unpredictable she could be, I said calmly, "Mum, these are two detectives and they're questioning me about a rape they think I might be involved in. They want to search my room, then they'll leave me alone. Right, detectives?"

Blue and Blondie nodded, looking at Mum whose face was becoming red with anger.

"Oh, is that all detectives?" she said. "Please come in, sure we're always raping people around here." When they started to enter, she suddenly began shouting at them. "Get out! Get out! Get out of my house!"

Fearing she might start beating them with a wooden spoon, I took her aside. "Mammy, let them in, otherwise they're going to lock me up in the police station. I want to get rid of them."

Seeing the sense in what I said, she finally agreed.

In searching my room, Blue found something he thought was very important. Tinfoil wrapped around a sizeable lump. Now in England we didn't smoke grass which I only learned about when I went to America. We smoked what people called 'shit' or 'hash,' which was burned with a lighter and crumbled into a joint with tobacco. When you weren't using your 'shit,' you stored it in tinfoil. This is what the brilliant Blue thought he'd discovered. Depending on the amount you had, you could get a hefty jail sentence. If he couldn't get me for rape, I thought, he might try to do me for drugs. I got that uneasy feeling again.

Slowly, carefully, he unwrapped the tinfoil, only to discover a different kind of drug, one used to satisfy the sweet tooth of the Irish. Chocolate. I'd wrapped up some leftover Cadburys Dairy Milk, with nuts in their trademark little squares.

"Would you like some, detective?" I said, ever so sweetly.

Blue was not amused. "Okay, we're done here, let's go," he said to Blondie.

As they left, Blue had the nerve to give me his card. "Call me anytime you think you have any useful information for me. We might want to talk you again, you're a person of interest."

As he went downstairs, I read his card and suddenly realised he wasn't what he purported to be. He wasn't a real cop at all, he was with the British Transport Police.

"You said you were a detective!"

"I am."

"But you're only a railway cop."

"We have exactly the same powers as the police, we can arrest anybody we suspect of wrong-doing."

When they were halfway down the stairs, I yelled, "You're only Railway Police... does that mean you know the Railway Children?" Then, on a more serious note, "I hope you find the person who did this terrible thing and that the poor woman recovers. But you shouldn't go around accusing people who are innocent." Blue shot me a look of anger, bordering on hatred.

When Dad came home, he too was angry and ready to call Blue

"Dad, there's something else I have to tell you," I said. "I keep a book that I write my dreams in. It's a bit rude. He might mention it."

"How rude?"

Knowing his love of James Joyce, I said, "Very rude, but not as bad as Molly's soliloquy in Ulysses!"

"Hmm," he sighed.

Based on Dad's retelling, this is how the conversation with Blue went.

"Detective, I hear you came to my house and searched my son's room. Did you have a search warrant?"

"Your son consented to a search. We didn't need one."

"My son said you threatened to arrest him if he didn't consent and put him in jail for the night."

Overhearing Blue's answer that this wasn't true, I said loudly, "He's lying, Dad."

"As you probably heard, my son says that's a lie. He also says he showed you his Post Office book which has an entry in it for the date you say the crime occurred. What exact time did the crime happen detective?"

Blue wouldn't tell him.

"Why can't you tell me, detective? Why is it such a big secret? Do I have to ask your superior officer and tell him about your shoddy police work? You harassed an innocent boy, you upset my wife and you illegally entered my house. My father was a high-ranking and respected police officer in Ireland, a Detective Chief Inspector and I've never heard of this kind of nonsense before."

Blue played his last card. "Have you seen what your son calls his dream book, sir? It has contents of a very sexual and disturbing nature. That's why he became a major suspect in this case. Your son also strongly resembles our artist's drawing of the culprit."

"Yes, he did tell me about his dream book. I believe he also told you about the psychiatrist Freud interpreting dreams. But it seems you were more interested in this book than his Post Office one which proves my son's whereabouts on the day in question."

Way to go, Dad. I was beaming with pride when he got off the phone.

Thinking about the incident many years later, I miss that cocky guy that was the younger me. He was fairly sure of himself and fairly fearless.

DREAMING OF AMERICA

As I wandered around picking up brown leaves from the ground using a mechanical device with two pincers at the end, I was daydreaming.

It was 1978 and I was a park attendant in Hull. I'd just finished college and knew there wasn't much for me there. In fact, Hull was the kind of town you didn't expect much from.

When I told the woman in the unemployment office I wanted a job, she was momentarily stunned, "What do you mean you want a job?" Half of Hull's citizens were unemployed and being on the dole was a way of life in this depressed northern town.

But not for me. I had a plan.

I was daydreaming about America and wondering what it would be like to live there.

At that time, Hull was the cheapest city in England. Though my salary wasn't high, my rent was so low I knew I'd be able to save up enough money in six months to gallivant around the States. I'd been intrigued by America most of my life and desperately wanted to go.

Amazingly enough, our college, which then had the reputation of being the worst art school in England, had an exchange program with the prestigious Fredonia College in upstate New York. Three students from Hull went to America every year to study and when I wasn't selected for the program, I was crushed. But it also turned my dream to go there into an obsession.

I had no idea what upstate New York meant. I thought it was some kind of pseudo-American name and I couldn't believe Fredonia students came from a college with the same name as the institution that had been so deliriously mocked by the Marx Brothers in the film, *'Hail, Hail Freedonia.'* As such, we found it hard to take them too seriously.

In turn, I think the Americans were shocked by Hull. Perhaps they were expecting an England of quaint people with funny accents. Instead the Yanks saw a city that looked like the Luftwaffe had just left. The reason was because old tenement housing was being demolished to usher in a 'brave new world' of desolate estates and high-rises. Therefore, most of Hull was destroyed, filled with what looked like bombed-out buildings in a war zone. There weren't even any student squatters because the local council in its wisdom had smashed all toilets and other plumbing utilities methodically in each building to discourage just that. Living space was hard to get for students so initially I shared a single bedroom with four other students.

Despite all this, we art students enjoyed being bohemian. All we needed in life was there, including the best fish and chips in the world and the greatest, cheapest beer in all of England courtesy of Hull Brewery whose hops' smell permeated the entire city.

RETURN TO IRELAND

When my parents finally decided to return to Ireland in 1975, I was shocked. After twenty odd years in England and always talking about going home, I thought it would never happen.

They'd put four sons through expensive fee-paying Catholic school plus boarding for years and they were broke. And as reciprocity had still not arrived, they were being paid less than their English counterparts in the chemist shops. Middle-class comfort had evaded them.

Back in Ireland, Mum quickly found a job in Kells, Meath and Dad in Dublin and after six months they rented a house in Monkstown, close to Dad's sisters, brother, nieces and nephews.

That's where troubles started. Their house was burgled, repeatedly - eleven times to be exact, twice in one day and once at night while they were asleep. So petrified were they, padlocks and bolts were put on each and every door in the house.

For the first time in their lives, my parents also bought a car. But that too was broken into, numerous times, and taken for joy rides. The innocent Dublin of their youth was long gone. Instead, the city was full of kids who'd rip you off, a significant number of them hard-core drug addicts. There were muggings in the street, something previously unheard of.

When I visited my parents, I noticed there was less bitter talk about the English than ever before. In fact, they spoke nostalgically about our previous life in the bucolic suburbs of London. Dad simply did not like this 'new Dublin' and missed the local pub in Ashtead, the brewery where he and I would meet his mates for a pint or two after Sunday mass.

In the end, my eldest brother Dave saved the day, loaning my parents enough money for a down-payment on a house in a quieter, safer area, in the shadow of the Wicklow Mountains. Here at last my parents found sanity.

MY FIRST DAY IN NEW YORK CITY

Not knowing much about America, having not been there before, my itinerary when I arrived in 1978 consisted of places my art college colleagues had gone to after winning their study grants.

Sedate Seattle was my first destination because I had a very good friend from school living there. Not only was it my first destination, it was also my first time seeing cops with guns at an airport, and my first time hearing the phrase, *"If life's a bowl of cherries, this sure is the pits,"* said by a woman on a downtown bus.

After Seattle, it was a whirlwind cross-country trip - via Greyhound bus for a full month - to California, Arizona, Colorado, Alabama, Massachusetts and New York.

I didn't mind the bus at all despite being told later by Americans it was the poor peoples' mode of transport. Compared to English busses, it was the height of luxury, including air conditioning, an on-time schedule, plentiful rest-stops and friendly staff.

And unlike stingy English cafes, in America I found out quick enough that I could refill my coffee endlessly for free and the food was not only good but came in huge portions. My first abiding impression of America was its sense of service. Here was a place you actually got what you paid for, and more.

My adventures in California and all points east had been fun, but chaste. Though I had a girlfriend back in England, we no longer lived together and had agreed '70s style to have an open relationship if either of us went away anywhere. Heading towards Massachusetts to see my last English contact, a boy called Chris, it looked as if I'd finish my trip with no romantic conquests whatsoever.

I didn't know Chris well. He'd been a year above me at school and I'd never talked to him very much. But when we met, he was so homesick we hit it off immediately as if we'd been the best of friends. We proceeded to have a really enjoyable time near the town of Northampton, hiking through local countryside, drinking in bars, and listening to Chris's eccentric English LPs such as Ivor Cutler's 'Dandruff.' But by sharing his very English tastes in the few days I was there, I think I may have made poor Chris even more homesick.

Anyway, with two days left on my visa and an airline ticket with my name on it from JFK Airport, I left Northampton and headed for the Big Apple. To many people in Britain, perhaps even worldwide, New York is the ultimate urban nightmare, teeming with crime and insanity. The Bronx was burning and you couldn't get on the subway without being mugged, or killed. Chris warned me I shouldn't go, describing it as "a cesspool." He worried about me leaving and when I wasn't in contact for a month afterwards, he thought I was dead. Instead, I was having one of the best times of my life.

Finally, I told Chris I had to go. Besides, I had contacts there. My older brother, Tim, had done the same thing as me, toured America on a Greyhound bus and then hit New York on his way out. While he was there, he'd met some artists at a bar whose loft he'd stayed in. Although he didn't rave about the city, he had told me it was fascinating, but warned me "to behave myself" if I stayed with his friends, Bob and Jenny, in the loft.

I arrived in New York on July 3, my bus pulling into the old Port Authority station on 34th Street, which reminded me of a station I knew in Marrakech, full of hustlers, people with dubious offers. Except the people here looked even more dangerous. As I'd done in Marrakech, I kept a vigilant eye on my bags and exited the station quickly.

My destination was an area called Tribeca where Bob and Jenny lived, but as I made my way along Eighth Avenue to the subway on a grim, rainy day, I heard a shot go off in the distance, followed by more, then volleys of them from different directions. My worst fears were confirmed. Chris had been right after all. New Yorkers were shooting at each other in the customary manner I'd read about in English newspapers.

The subway at Times Square only confirmed my pre-conceptions about the city. It looked like the arsehole of the world. The station was filthy, the arriving subway cars covered in graffiti and not with the urban masterpieces I'd been led to believe. The people themselves seemed to be uniformly grey and unfriendly, obviously expecting to be murdered at any minute. I made it safely downtown to Canal Street and went looking for Lispenard Street in Tribeca. I could still hear shots going off all over town but thankfully it didn't seem to be quite as near and I was soon relieved to see that Tribeca looked a lot more sedate than Times Square.

Number 53 Lispenard was beside a strangely-named restaurant, 'Rachel Street Jewish Soul Food.' I wondered what that could possibly be as I went upstairs to the much-vaunted loft. Bob and Jenny were older than me, in their early 30s, he already balding. After introducing myself as Tim's brother, Jenny greeted me with an incredulous, "Who? Teem who?" Neither of them seemed to have the faintest idea who Tim was.

Jenny spoke with the most amazingly squeaky voice I'd ever heard, like that of a cartoon character.

"Tim Mara," I said.

A long silence ensued, and I thought maybe I had the wrong address. Then finally, "Oh Teemy Mara! You remember him, Bob. Teemy."

Tim had never been called this in his life. Or

else he'd invented a whole new identity for himself in New York.

Bob spoke with a voice straight out of the first Rocky movie, "Yo, Tim Mara, a great English artist. Yeah, of course, Tim. Welcome, would you like a highball?"

I'd heard of highballs, of course. You saw people in old movies drinking them in Manhattan, but I wasn't exactly sure what it was. I replied, "Arms could be twisted."

This elicited a giggle from Jenny who had warmed to me now that she knew who I was. I prepared to toast the seemingly legendary Maras of New York City. After three of these concoctions, I began to feel quite happy and was glad I'd dropped by. By this time, all three of us were getting on like a house on fire.

As you tend do with Americans during your first meeting, I quickly learned Bob and Jenny's life stories. Bob had been in Vietnam and, having seen a lot of action, nothing scared him anymore. He wore a pair of black combat boots which I assumed were straight from there and now dedicated his life to his adopted motto 'art for the people,' seemingly to help make up for whatever misadventures he'd had in Vietnam. His activities involved his art group, called 'Ken's Fellas' which hosted community events such as open-air barbecues featuring art exhibitions and performing artists of all kinds. In fact, the very next day was to be their annual 'Ken's Fellas' barbecue in Tribeca. Large supplies of beer were on hand which we proceeded to drink to wash down the highballs, Bob calling this combination, 'boilermakers.'

Jenny was from New Mexico and she and Bob had been high-school sweethearts. She was also devoted to the cause of art. As we talked, various people popped in introducing themselves as artists and asked me what I did. I didn't really consider myself an artist, just an ex-art student. In England, you weren't a real artist unless you were making money from it full-time or had a position as a tutor at an art college like my brother. Anybody else was considered a poser or a wanker. I said I made films. Seeing as I'd just graduated college, I felt justified in saying this. Bob felt I could be useful to 'Ken's Fellas' as a documentarian for future activities, as a PR guy.

It all seemed to be a lot of fun compared to the snobby world of English art back home. I was announced more as a visiting international artist than a bloke at the end of his holidays who'd just stopped in to say hello before returning to England. Within a matter of hours of arriving, I was rapidly becoming a bona fide New York celebrity, something that would never have happened in England due to the class-conscious nature of society there. I was enjoying myself tremendously and stayed up late talking and drinking, happily looking forward to the next day and my new role as an international member of 'Ken's Fellas.'

MY SECOND DAY IN NEW YORK

When morning came, we headed down to
Battery City, lugging our supplies for the barbecue -
beer kegs, hamburgers, hot dogs and gear to set up a
food stall. It was physically demanding work, but I
was eager to enhance my reputation as an essential
cog in Ken's collective.

At the park, various festivities for the Fourth of
July were already underway including fireworks
going off every ten seconds or so. Unlike English
fireworks, they were incredibly loud rather than being
showy. I was informed that most of the fireworks
were M-80s which could blow a person's hand off if
held too long. Then it dawned on me. All those
gunshots I thought I'd heard since my arrival in the
city had, in fact, been fireworks. With relief, I turned
back to my hamburger duties.

I'd recently worked on another brother's
hamburger stall at a London market so I was quite a
dab hand at it. Bob and the assembled crew were

impressed. Here was a Brit who'd turned up out of the blue and was showing the best way to cook a burger.

There were a few surprises that day. One customer, a woman, wanted a hot dog and asked was it possible to put some garlic on it because, "normally I put garlic up my vagina because of its holistic qualities but I don't have any with me." I replied that we didn't have garlic, adding that despite garlic's holistic qualities maybe it wasn't such a good idea to insert it into her vagina because it might taste funny. She gave me a puzzled look and walked away. I don't think she understood my sense of humor. But it was still fantastic, a complete stranger walking up to me and discussing her intimate organs in the very first sentence.

I couldn't wait to see what New York had in store for me next. Secretly, I was hoping it would be Suzy, one of 'Ken's Fellas' helpers on the hamburger stand with me. An attractive 30-ish divorcee, she was vivacious, a fantasy come true, a movie star with gleaming white teeth and a broad, friendly smile. They didn't make English girls like this, I thought. In short, she was as sexy as hell. She reminded me of that Rolling Stones line 'I mettuh, divorsay in Noo Yawk City… she tried to take me upstairs fuh a ride…'

"You handled that really well," she said, amused at how I'd dealt with the vagina lady. I would have liked to have replied Bogey-like, "Yes, and I think I could handle you very well too if you just give me a chance." But of course I didn't.

As she spoke she was bouncing a small rubber ball up and down on the concrete. Unbelievable! A gorgeous woman, the woman of my dreams, playing with a rubber ball and flirting with me at a hamburger stand in New York City.

Suddenly, somebody came between us, another figure intruding on our private-island-hamburger-hot-dog-garlic-up-my-vagina stand. His name was Bill and, as I'd already learned, he was Suzy's recent ex-boyfriend. One of Ken's fellow Vietnam vets, he was a little hostile.

"Why don't you two really get to know each other, eh?" He grabbed us by the back of our necks and slammed us into each other so we were almost kissing. I didn't really mind that much. I was now really close to Suzy and I saw by her expression she didn't mind too much either. Thank you, Bill.

Later that night we went down to Little Italy to soak up the atmosphere. The sidewalks were crowded, some being tourists but many others as well, with their swept back jet black hair, local Italian American men. On Mulberry Street these men had placed a smorgasbord of fireworks on a pile of discarded wood that appeared ready for a bonfire. Didn't they know how dangerous this was? Apparently not, because one of the young men stepped forward and lit the heaped pile. Boom! The fireworks exploded in all directions sending people, scurrying into the doorways of Italian restaurants as fiery rockets whizzed in all directions. Some people actually threw more fireworks on to the pile. I'd never seen anything like it. Our Guy Fawkes celebrations in England were nothing like this.

Maybe because of all the excitement, Suzy needed to go to the bathroom urgently. So, without a word, she stepped discreetly behind a dumpster. Luckily, so noisy and frantic was the scene around us, no-one noticed. I guarded her activity virtuously.

Later that night we went back to her place, a basement apartment on Crosby Street, with metal gates that looked like a delivery entrance. Suzy was everything I expected and more. I was falling in love on my second day in New York City. What else lay ahead?

MY THIRD DAY IN NEW YORK CITY

The next morning Bob came by, but Suzy and I were still in bed. Life is short and happiness elusive, so I wanted to stay in bed all day, possibly for the rest of my life. My brother had told me to behave myself and now look what I was up to.

In the end, we dressed reluctantly and headed downtown. A routine errand, Bob said, to sort out a bit of machinery. I didn't care what it was. I was deliriously and madly in love. Nothing else mattered. As we were crossing a green light on Canal Street, a car turned right across our path, stopping us in our tracks. It was the American Cadillac of my movie dreams. As the car cut across us, Bob gave it a swift kick. In fact, kicked it so hard with his Vietnam boots, he made a dent in it. The Cadillac stopped and out stepped a tall, angry black man as if straight out of the crime drama, Superfly, wearing a fedora, boots and a fancy shirt.

"What the fuck you doin,' motherfucker?"

Motherfucker? I was being addressed as a motherfucker in New York a mere day after arriving. We have some tough swear words in England but to me this was the most heinous curse I'd ever heard.

Bob was genuinely shocked and said to me, "Keep walking. Ignore him."

But how could I? The man was following us down the street, all the while calling us motherfuckers. New York was crazy after all, I thought. I was going to die right here on the spot just like everybody had warned me.

The man continued shouting, "yo motherfuckers, cocksuckers." At one point, Bob asked me if the man was still following us as we didn't dare look around in case we provoked him further.

"Yeah," I whispered out of the side of my mouth.

Then I tried to put some distance between Bob and myself. After all, he'd caused the whole situation and my loyalty to a madman is rather limited.

Thankfully, after a couple of blocks, the man gave up the chase. I was relieved but Bob just winked at me, a wicked smile on his lips. Without further incident, we arrived at our destination on Canal Street, a parts depot. Bob produced a plastic bag with a spare part in it, a tiny cog whose function to me was unknown. He then proceeded to tell the shopkeeper a story about how he'd purchased the cog for $1.79. I was expecting the same courteous service I'd experienced elsewhere in America but it turned out much different.

"Are you shitting me?" the guy asked Bob incredulously. Get outa' here!"

Are you shitting me? I hadn't heard those words in all my years of retail shopping in England. It turned out Bob had the wrong store, so off we went, to the right one. Except now it turned out Bob had purchased the item not last Christmas but the Christmas before.

"Why don't you get the fuck outa' of here?" the guy behind the counter said simply,

"So you don't wan' it?" Bob muttered.

"I don't wan' it," was the reply.

"Well if you don't wan' it, then I don't wan' it," retorted Bob. Then he flung the cog against the wall behind the assistant. As he did so something unexpected happened. A hulking bear of a bald man rushed up the stairs from the basement and grabbed Bob by his lapels.

"Where you from? Moscow?" he yelled.

"Yeah, I'm from Moscow, so don' fuckin' touch' me!" Bob replied.

A pseudo-sumo wrestling match then began between them with each shouting at the other, either "get the fuck offa me" or "get the fuck outa' here." Eventually the bald man tossed us both out of the shop, ably assisted by his colleague who waved a crowbar in the air menacingly. Back on bustling Canal Street, Bob looked at me and smiled, "pretty funny, huh!" I was completely flummoxed, but bit my lip, remembering my older brother's advice about 'good behaviour.'

Over the next few days there were other 'pretty funny' incidents with Bob and Jenny in just about every public service centre we went to. In a supermarket, Jenny argued loudly with a sales girl about a discounted lettuce. I couldn't believe it. As an irate queue grew longer at the check-out counter, the manager was called. After much haggling, eventually Jenny won her few cents. Outside, Bob and Jenny agreed on the righteousness of their cause. I said nothing. It slowly dawned on me that they held an obstinate belief they were always right and that the world owed them. But then again, what did I know?

Yet another telling incident took place when we went to John's Pizza, made famous in Woody Allen movies.

"Er yo, if you're giving us more water it has to be in new ones," said Bob, stopping a waiter who was about to refill our glasses.

"You're kidding, right?" the waiter replied.

"No, it's the law in New York, you have to have new glasses," said Jenny.

"Let me talk to the manager," was all the waiter could manage as he backed away from the table from hell.

An older guy called John came over. "What's the problem?"

Jenny began to explain to him about the law. In Italian.

At first, John seemed reasonable but next thing I knew they were screaming at each other, with Jenny occasionally reverting back to English. By now, the entire restaurant had turned to see what was happening, having absolutely no idea what was going on. Eventually, John smiled, "OK, so you want clean glasses? I give you a clean glasses."

Taking the offending glasses away he disappeared into the kitchen as Bob and Jenny looked at each other in a self-congratulating way. Returning with sparkling glasses and filling them from the pitcher, John said simply, " 'appy?" Bob and Jenny nodded their silent agreement.

THE REST OF MY DAYS IN NEW YORK CITY

Strange as these situations might have been with Bob and Jenny, I was still having a wonderful time in New York and decided to extend my stay for a month. I was young, confident, happy, and in love. And I also had a job.

First, I helped a friend of Bob's build a raised floor in a shoe shop. Then I took a job as a waiter at the 'Rachel Street Jewish Soul Food' restaurant, owned by a woman called Rachel. The wages were fantastic compared to England, forty to fifty dollars a day - twice if not three times what I might earn back home. Plus, living was cheaper in New York. A good breakfast was fifty cents, a quarter in some places. And there were enormous hero sandwiches for lunch the likes of which I'd never seen before and if that didn't suit your palate there was always a slice of glorious pizza. New York was truly paved with gold, great cheap food and steaming hot sex.

Rachel was delighted with my English accent and explained what my duties would be while also, strangely, telling me a lot about her psychiatrist. She said she'd have to pay for an extra session with him if I didn't take the job and relieve her stress. I dutifully accepted, much to her delight, but wondered if I had entered a Woody Allen movie.

Tribeca was largely undiscovered then, the restaurant was small and very few people came, most of them being Rachel's friends. I began to learn about borscht, blintzes and dumplings called pierogis. Rachel introduced me as the 'dynamite waiter, fresh from England' At 21, I didn't mind at all.

Rachel, however, was constantly fighting with the chef. He was good at his job but she simply didn't like him, so she fired him. Then, much to my surprise, she asked me to take his place, promising me she'd teach me how to cook. I was hesitant at first, of course, but because I was so happy, I said yes. I was in love and felt I could do anything. Bob and the rest of my New York gang thought it hilarious.

So, there I was in my white apron, working with the only other employee, Peter, a glorified bottle-washer, who was also Rachel's nephew. Older than me, about 30, swarthy, with black hair topped by a yarmulke at the crown, he seemed slow, as if walking through a fog, but he wasn't so slow not to operate his own secret pay-out system. Out of every five dollars that went into the till I saw him brazenly put two in his pocket. Rachel didn't seem to notice, or care.

For about a week, everything went fine, except for the occasional exploding pierogi dumpling or blintz in the frying pan. Then one day a calamity occurred as I was preparing food before opening. I'd made pierogis and blintzes in two huge bowls when Rachel arrived and began screaming, "What have you done?"

I was mystified. Putting her hands in the bowls, she yelled, "You've fucked up."

I looked at the soggy pierogis in her hands, they were stuck together like glue. "It's OK," I said. "I'll separate them, slowly."

"You can't, they're fucking stuck."

I tried to extricate the interlocked pierogis. But she was right, it was hopeless, they were one big glutinous mass.

"You fucked up, we're opening in five minutes, what am I going to do? Tell the customers I have no food because you fucked up?"

We managed to get through the evening ok but despite Rachel's entreaties, including her threat of a nervous breakdown and additional sessions with her psychiatrist, I quit. There's only so much craziness you can take, plus it was time to go home.

So, that was it, my adventures in America were finally over. At the end of July I said sad goodbyes to Bob, Jenny, tearful Suzy and the whole crew.

BACK STATESIDE AGAIN

I missed what I'd call the 'mad excitement' of New York and it wasn't long until I was back, leaving England behind for good.

It was 1981 and here I was living in an abandoned restaurant, called L and M, on Hudson Avenue, Vinegar Hill, Brooklyn.

I had noticed the place vacant when I'd come on a visit from London to Julian, a Lithuanian–American artist friend who lived only two doors down from it.

The storefront was spacious and my idea was that Julian could take half as his studio, leaving me the other half. Corresponding cross-Atlantic by letter, I told Julian I'd come over soon and would get a job quickly if he could acquire the place for us to rent.

In its heyday, L and M had done well, serving up diner fare: pastrami on rye, BLTs, breakfast with eggs, sausages, hash fries, pancakes, coffee and anything else you might want. But now it was city-owned and Julian worked diligently on the complicated paperwork to get us the property. Rent was the princely sum of $112, very cheap even then, and soon after I moved in I got a construction job in Brooklyn Heights on a Korean church. Work was plentiful in New York in those days, off the books with the pay being much higher than comparable jobs in England.

Next door to L and M was 'Jimmy's,' a bar-cum-deli with red neon beer signs in the window and an air-conditioner jutting out front. With L and M gone, Jimmy catered almost exclusively to workers at the local Con Ed plant

Italian-American, Jimmy made fantastic meatball and eggplant heroes amongst other delights. Part of a small Italian group in the neighbourhood who still owned some bars and delis, he worked like a demon. Years before, he told me, when the Brooklyn Navy Yard a mile up the street employed thousands of workers, Hudson Avenue was known as 'Chicken Broadway' and was choc-a-bloc with cheap hotels, bustling bars and lively ladies of the night. By the time I got to Vinegar Hill, it was a Lithuanian neighbourhood and Julian fitted in perfectly, his parents being from Lithuania and he speaking the language like a native.

The avenue was full of colourful characters. Like 'Mad Jake' for example. Middle-aged and lonely since his parents died, he'd shout loudly throughout the night in his house at no-one in particular. If he was too loud, all you had to do was tell him to shut up and he usually did.

I loved the elderly Lithuanians who, in their

turn, didn't mind us newcomers. We were young, respectful and we'd help them out if they needed anything. I also became enamoured of their culture and customs. I've had Christmas with Lithuanians where venison was served as well as the craziest of New Year's dinners when a piglet's head ended up flying across the room.

Two characters who did a lot for the neighbourhood were a gay couple called Dan and Mike. They were heavily involved in a campaign to prevent the city paving Vinegar Hill with ugly blacktop, saying it would destroy the area's *'old world charm.'* Their efforts meant the district still has a beautifully cobblestoned street. Sadly, Dan fell victim to AIDS. I'm not sure what happened to Mike, I certainly hope it was a kinder fate.

The original artists who moved into Vinegar Hill, Soho, Tribeca and Williamsburg transformed run-down areas into their own private havens. Half of New York was built by artists living off-the-books for decades in lofts, storefronts and abandoned buildings of all kinds. They did it so well, of course, that smooth real estate agents and developers came later, eventually forcing most of them out. The world where people came to New York to be artists and took jobs as construction workers, waiters and bartenders and did their art in their spare time in fairly cheap apartments or lofts, no longer exists. All in all, I thoroughly enjoyed my lifestyle on Vinegar Hill.

That is, until Val entered the picture.

DRUG DEALING AND A SILVER GUN

It was 1984 and I was still living in the converted storefront. Rent-controlled and cheap, it was worth hanging on to. But there was one little problem.

Val, my upstairs neighbour, was running a drugs business, supplying the bad boys from the projects two blocks up the street and anybody else who was interested. He even had a kid as a lookout on my stoop.

In this once Irish, now Lithuanian district, there had always been a small Italian presence. What remained was a low-level but friendly mafioso. The local grocery store, for example, was run by a fella called Tony who also indulged in the numbers game and few other minor illegal activities. His store stood on the demarcation line between the projects and the artist's colony just down the street where I lived. Tony was a friendly character with a reputation for keeping things 'cool' in the neighbourhood. Both Tony and

Val were best friends, with Val often seen carrying his Adidas sports bag around with him after a day's work dealing drugs, ready for a game of squash with his pal.

Val also saw himself as an unelected public servant to the community. In this capacity one Spring day, he had a black limousine pull up outside my place and out stepped four voluptuous black girls in high heels, furs and outrageous wigs that hadn't been in fashion since The Supremes. All day and well into the evening, Con Edison workers from the nearby plant ran up and down the stairs like excited school children, causing a bit of pandemonium on an otherwise quiet street. I later learned Val had offered a generous discount to the Con Ed workers, for what is best termed 'services rendered.'

Since then, however, things had gone downhill. Instead of the sporty, racquet-carrying drug dealer and pimp of yesteryear, Val had become the neighborhood's answer to the ageing Las Vegas Elvis. He'd gotten fat and his weight seemed unnatural, like inflated air. His demeanour was unfriendly and he seemed in a permanent daze. His drug business was booming, his client's loud comings and goings at all hours driving my neighbours and I crazy.

Previous to this, I'd gotten too cosy with Val than I should have. One night, six months earlier, he had come downstairs seeking a favor.

"Can you look after this for me for a few minutes?" he said pointing to his Adidas sports bag. "My power is out and I can't see what I'm doing."

Seeing my apprehension, he added, "It's cool, I'm just waiting for someone to pick this up."

Reluctantly, I agreed, realising Val wasn't asking me, he was telling me. Then he disappeared upstairs, anxiously looking over his shoulder as he left. I waited in the apartment with the Adidas bag by the front door for half an hour, making sure I double-locked. That's when I began to wonder. What would happen if the police raided my building? If this surprisingly heavy bag contained what I thought it did and was found in my apartment, I could go to jail for five to ten years. Would Val help me out? Doubtful.

Terrible scenes involving Riker's Island flashed through my mind.

I went upstairs to Val. "Look," I said through his closed door "I really don't want anything to do with this. You've got to take this bag back now." Val agreed, saying he'd come downstairs in a minute.

When he did, to my horror, he placed the bag on my kitchen table and took out a huge plastic container filled with cocaine. He then insisted I take twenty dollars for my trouble. I refused. The last thing I wanted was to be indebted to Val.

"Is this place secure?" he suddenly asked, gazing towards my back window.

"Yeah," I replied not having the heart to tell him the window was only covered by a plastic sheet.

"Good," he said. "That's good."

Then, taking one of my oven trays, he proceeded to open the cocaine bag and deposit its contents on it until it seemed like a snow-covered model of Mount Rushmore.

"Seeing as you won't take money, here's a little something for your trouble," he said, cutting a small portion of the white powder with a kitchen knife. Had he computed precisely twenty dollars of coke in the slicing?

After he left, which wasn't soon enough for me, I pondered what I'd just done. What did this mean about my future relationship with Val? I'd never been a druggie, preferring a pint of Guinness any day. I could hold a beer or two but I couldn't hold a joint. I threw up everywhere, parties, social events, wherever. In fact, I'd become famous, or should I say, infamous, for it. Pot made me feel paranoiac, sweaty and nauseous, all at the same time. I hadn't smoked dope in ten years and I'd never even tried cocaine until I'd come to America. It just wasn't easily available in England in the early 80's. Anyway, I considered it an American rich kid's drug and therefore bourgeoisie and my English socialist heart didn't like the idea of that.

Now, staring at Val's cocaine, I wondered if it would be any different this time. Not knowing the etiquette of snorting, I proceeded as I'd seen it done in the movies. A flat surface for a mirror but with a single straw instead of a hundred-dollar bill. I snorted the first line. Ahh. Instantly all my problems dissolved. The world was wonderful. Everything was crystal clear, perfectly so. I don't think I've ever felt so happy in my entire life. This was better than sex and required no effort at all. I fully realised why people became addicted to this drug. I finished the other lines and looked at myself in the mirror. What I saw was a demented, shit-eating grin of a face, with asterisks for eyes.

I've never had a narcotic high like that. Nor did I ever let Val use my place for any kind of illicit storage again. I was ashamed he'd been able to pay me off with cocaine. I didn't want to be part of the problem and the problem was getting worse. Val was now terrorising the elderly couple directly above me as the scum of the earth traipsed endlessly upstairs to his apartment. Sometimes, when I came home late at night, his head would pop out from his window. Paranoid, he'd ask who I was and what business did I have in the neighbourhood.

There was no point telling city officials who came around asking if there were any 'undesirables or drug dealers in the building' about Val. If I had, the city would probably have sent him an eviction notice mentioning that the tenant downstairs, Joseph Mara, had complained about his activities. Also, Val rented his apartment through one of his paisans, Maria, who worked for the Brooklyn office of the Housing Department.

Val now gave me hostile stares whenever we'd meet on the street. Where was this all going to end? I thought. I soon found out. Late one evening, there was a rat-a-tat-tat on my door. When I opened it, he was there.

"Have you seen Jim?" he asked. Jim was an artist buddy of mine who'd lived next door for the last six years.

"No," I replied with English-style sarcasm. "Jim lives next door, has always lived next door. This is my place."

"You show me no respect," Val suddenly screamed. "I've been twenty fuckin' years in this neighbourhood, long before you motherfucker." He gestured outside to the street, "I own this fuckin' street, this fuckin' neighborhood and I own you too. You're the mother-fucker who told the cops on me aren't you? I'll blow you away."

He started to push his way into my apartment, putting his hand under his armpit as if he had a gun. Not knowing if he was armed or not, I backed off. He'd kill me if he thought I'd tipped off the cops.

"Val, I didn't tell the cops," I replied, feeling very uneasy.

"Whether you did or didn't," he said, still angry. "If you don't show me no fuckin' respect in this neighbourhood, I'll waste you."

It was obvious I had to get out of the apartment as soon as possible. I could move next door to another apartment, for a lot more money, but at least I'd be alive. Two weeks later I did. And Jim moved into my place. Val must have thought I still lived there because the apartment was burglarised a week later as Jim was sleeping. I assumed Val paid one of his junkie customers to do it. Luckily, Jim woke up.

"Who the fuck's there?" he demanded, shining a light on the intruder.

"Nobody man," was all the intruder said. "Have

you seen Val?" Then he jumped out through the plastic window.

Next day, Jim asked Val what was going on and was told it was all a misunderstanding. Then he showed Jim a new toy he'd gotten, a silver-colored, 38-caliber revolver which he said he'd used to keep 'undesirables' like me out of the neighbourhood. I may have been gone from my apartment but obviously not gone far enough.

LIVING WITH THE LITHUANIANS

The people I'd rented my new apartment from were an elderly Lithuanian couple, Johnny-on- the-Spot, as he was known, and his wife, Stella.

I liked Lithuanians. My favorites were Veronica, my friend Jim's landlady, and Edward, an aging vagabond lush known variously as the Gypsy or the Shadow. Edward worked in the bar next door sweeping floor and spending the little money he earned on liquor and occasional young Puerto Rican girls. In his mid-60's, he was still good-looking with a twinkle in his eye despite the fact he was virtually homeless. Veronica was about 70 and grew marijuana in her backyard for medicinal purposes just like her family did back home in Lithuania. She was a good Christian woman but hated Russians and Communism.

Some of the flowers Veronica planted only opened at night. I think they were called Moonflowers and she'd make up all sorts of Old World herbal remedies from them. Once when I was violently sick for two weeks with flu-like symptoms and diarrhea, she dosed me with a strange-looking liquid containing berries, leaves and twigs. It cured me overnight. Next day I woke feeling as right as rain. With winter coming, out of the goodness of her heart she'd let Edward the Shadow stay in her basement as long as he behaved himself. Unknown to her, he still smuggled young girls down there whenever he could, usually when Veronica went out to feed pigeons in the parking lot opposite. Wearing her wild black and white polka dot dress, she spoke Lithuanian to them as Edward carried on back in her basement.

Johnny-on-the-Spot and Stella were quite different. Their nature was much more vindictive and gossipy. But at least, they were easier to deal with than Val. Johnny's left shoe had a hole in it and all his toes poked out. Maybe the foot needed air, for it was permanently air-conditioned. Johnny had acquired his nickname because he always seemed to be there when you turned around. If you opened a door to go outside, Johnny would invariably be on the other side. I soon realised they were the most obsessive snoopers I'd ever come across. They were pathological and, in turn, made me somewhat pathological.

My apartment was great. It was big, luxurious and I was happy. Johnny and Stella implied that I could become their new object of affection after they had previously evicted Stella's sister and her family. I could be their newfound son. I might even inherit their house, they said.

But being a good boy wasn't easy. It meant

catering to their every whim. For a few weeks, there was a brief honeymoon as I replaced locks on doors, laid down cement for a patio floor, all the things that a dutiful son does. But they were unpredictable. One day, after Jim had assembled a sculpture resembling a nuclear bomb on the parking lot for an art show, Johnny walked calmly over, doused it with gasoline and set a match to it. It lit up the evening sky like a barn fire. Jim was philosophical about it, reckoning Johnny had improved his piece, turning it into kinetic art with rare conceptual possibilities.

Meanwhile, regarding my own artistic aspirations. A friend had donated a green 16-millimeter moviola machine to me for a film project. It must have weighed around five hundred pounds and, with its forest of take-up reel arms, resembled a giant industrial green octopus. With the help of two friends, I smuggled it into my apartment when Johnny and Stella were away.

Everything I now did was done in secret, whether that was having guests over or getting to my mail first before Johnny and Stella read it. Once, a postcard arrived for me from friends in England who were coming to visit me. As I spent most weekends with my girlfriend, Roe, in Rockaway Beach, I made the mistake of giving Johnny and Stella her phone number in case of an emergency. Johnny called me up and read the entire postcard over the phone, then asked if I knew the exact day when my friends would be visiting. I asked facetiously if they'd put a date on the postcard. Johnny paused to look, then without a trace of irony told me no.

Despite all this madness, Johnny, Stella and I would occasionally watch baseball games together as I'd recently become a convert to the sport and they were diehard Mets fans. The Mets had signed a new pitcher, Doc Gooden, and were hot again after years in the wilderness.

But my days of being 'their boy' were coming to an end.

Johnny and Stella were snooping in my apartment when I was away and discovered the moviola machine, viewing it with horror, a technological monster which, when plugged in, would consume their house with fire like a dragon breathing flames. They'd even invited Dario, the local bar owner, to see 'the monster' and to give his independent opinion, which strongly echoed their own. In short, the beast would burn down their house through an electrical overload and possibly the entire block. With this testimonial in hand and their indefinable logic, they left me a note. Either I went, or the machine did.

Angry about invading my privacy, I made a hasty and serious blunder. I replied to their note with a retaliatory one of my own, telling them I was keeping the machine and that I didn't need any technical advice from 'their scummy mafiosi friends.' They spitefully showed the note to Dario who gave me the evil eye whenever we'd meet in the street. Jim told me I was mad. Didn't I know Dario was one of Val's close friends?

There was only one thing to do, I would have to apologize to Dario. I went into the bar when it wasn't too busy and asked to speak to him. On one wall was a picture of Marlon Brando in *'The Godfather,'* with the caption below reading, *'I'm gonna' make you an offer you can't refuse.'*

I apologised to Dario and he replied like a stock character from a movie, "Why do you say these terrible things about me? I was only trying to help. I know Johnny and Stella aren't all there but they're old so what're you gonna' do? Vallie isn't like he used to be either, but that's why you gotta' be careful of him. He's gettin' a little crazy. Says you're always causing trouble in the neighborhood."

Val might actually now decide to kill me, I thought, not just for disrespecting him, but insulting his friend. I felt it would be wise to move even further from the neighborhood.

The 'monster' went a week later and I followed shortly afterwards. It was a Saturday and there was a party atmosphere on the block as I packed all my belongings into Jim's pickup. Veronica was there toasting me with grappa as well as Edward the Shadow and several other neighbours who helped load up. The only people not at the party were Johnny and Stella who glared at me from their top floor window.

Occasionally, much later, I went back to the old neighbourhood. Veronica had suffered a heart attack and died on her kitchen floor and somebody else now owns the building. She never lived to see Lithuania independent and free of the hated Russians. Johnny and Stella are both dead too. Johnny went first, I hope they gave him a good left shoe wherever he went. Stella must have been desperately lonely for he was in perfect sync with her madness. Jim told me she died from heart failure shortly after Con Edison began tearing up the parking lot in front of her house with huge caterpillars to make a new plant. Jim said all the houses on the block shook while the work was being done. So, in the end, it was a different kind of technological monster that tore up the earth under Stella's feet.

Val was busted by a SWAT team late one night and 'sent up river' for about five years. I hope he didn't think it was I who informed on him. Edward the Shadow lived briefly in Jim's basement in a crude kind of shanty-town apartment with a black and white television. The last time I saw the Shadow in the neighbourhood it reminded me of an incident that had happened a few years earlier.

One morning Jim had come to see me. "Look at this," he said, handing me an envelope. It had a weird looking foreign stamp and postmark on it. Inside was a photograph and a letter. The photo looked like it was taken in the '40s or '50s. A stout man wearing a grey suit stood next to a Christmas tree with adults and children in the background. The man looked relatively prosperous and comfortable. It was Edward the Shadow. The letter was written in stilted English but basically read, *We are writing to you about a man called Edward Navickas who left Lithuania in*

1952 and went to New York. We know he lived at this address. We're trying to get in touch with him as we haven't heard from him in about twenty years. We would be grateful if you know who the man is in the photo to please contact us. We are his family, he is our uncle.'

It was signed Kasimir Navickas. So Edward had a family and somehow had gotten lost or shipwrecked in New York. Who knew what had transpired during the intervening years?

Later that day, Jim gave the envelope to Edward who went quiet when he saw the photo and walked away. We didn't see Edward for a couple of days. Usually we hung out on the stoop with him during the summer, sharing beers. A week later he was back as if nothing had happened. Jim and I never mentioned the letter to him again. If we'd had any sense, we could have kept his relatives' address and written to them giving diplomatic information about Edward's condition and whereabouts. But now it was too late.

Many years later, I saw Edward on a visit to my old neighbourhood. He was standing outside muttering incoherently as he drank a can of beer out of a brown bag. I realised he didn't know who I was. His eyes and cheek-bones had sunk in, making his face resemble a skull and he had grey stubble on his face. There was no twinkle about him anymore.

I also went to Dario's bar. He was no longer there as the place had changed ownership. The Marlon Brando poster, however, was still on the wall offering the same deal I couldn't refuse.

ALI AND ME

Ali was a filmmaker friend of mine from art college in England who'd been accepted to New York University's film school and moved over in 1978.

Iranian, he was a man of the world. Urbane, suave, sophisticated. He spoke English fluently, as well as Farsi, had a black belt in karate, and was a great cook. He'd often hold big dinner parties where he'd play his favorite jazz like Chico Hamilton, Oscar Peterson and Chick Corea.

While in Hull, after finishing my day as a park attendant, I'd sometimes walk over to his apartment, which was often packed with college friends holding large glasses of vodka in one hand and large joints in the other.

Ali became very busy after moving to New York, working on various projects so we didn't see much of each other. I recall vividly, however, one occasion meeting him at the university. Seeing a black man in a side room frantically winding large sixteen millimeter reels of film through a moviola, I asked who it was. "Oh, that's Spike Lee," Ali replied nonchalantly. Film-makers Jim Jarmusch and the Coen brothers were also at NYU at that time.

After several years in America, my cultural tastes had changed dramatically. I'd gone off high art, especially French neo-existential movies, and had become a hard-boiled detective/film noir fan. Ali still retained his interest in foreign art-house movies and dragged me out to see a new Italian film, *'Leap Into The Void.'* I fell asleep during it, which I rarely do. All I could remember was that at some point a man was standing on top of an office desk urinating on it and when I woke up the same man was leaping out of a window to his death. Ali loved the movie, having already seen it several times.

Afterwards, with a woman I'd just started dating called Roe, we walked to his house in Chelsea for a few drinks where we discussed the movie. I said I didn't get it and Ali said he thought I was becoming a real cultural hardhead, something I was secretly proud of. My new girlfriend and Ali, however, discussed the movie animatedly. Once, when she left the room, Ali said, "I like her." They'd formed an immediate bond and I've often thought since that Ali liked Roe much more than me.

Ali graduated from NYU in 1982 and found freelance work as a film editor. While his day job was as a clerk in an Iranian bank, he'd been given a lot of leeway to pursue his true interests. A year later, he quit his bank job and moved in with me in Vinegar

Hill. As he'd left unconditionally, he had no steady income, so he sublet his apartment in the city. He'd first arranged to stay with a cousin living in Queens but that didn't work out so he ended up on my sofa for four months.

Although we were practically living on top of each other, Ali was the perfect guest, knowing when to disappear and reappear, and always the gentleman. As I was unemployed almost as much as he, we spent a lot of time together. We played endless chess games and talked, talked and talked some more. Ali, ever so proud, would pass on film work to me that he considered low paying or simply beneath him. He also had a lot of close women friends but his personal relationships seemed complicated, with some describing him as intense and moody, almost morbid. Though not classically handsome, he had a gentle and inviting look which many women found attractive. He was a very private person and guarded his affairs closely, so we never discussed personal issues. Once at a party, however, he became very drunk and proposed to a woman on bended knee. Her boyfriend, a friend of mine, stood by, grinning.

Film work in New York City in winter was slow and I knew Ali was broke. But being so proud, in February 1985 he gave me a strange gift for my wedding at which he was best man. His finest jacket. It was almost the only thing he had left to give.

Eventually Ali returned to Manhattan where he worked on PBS documentaries and low-budget independent films. He had been seeing a Chinese woman, June, for quite a while, until they broke up. But through a mutual friend I found out she was pregnant and was keeping the baby against his wishes. Penniless, but the perfect gentleman, Ali insisted June move in with him.

Later, after finding a job on an independent film, he tried to get me hired as a dailies sync editor. I wasn't qualified but I went for the interview anyway. It was a horror movie and post-production was taking place in a huge loft in Times Square. I didn't get the job but what I saw of it featured a semi-nude teenage girl being bloodily murdered in a shower by a knife-wielding maniac. In artistic terms, it was a long way from *'Leap Into The Void.'*

Meanwhile, Ali confided in me that a young female NYU student, an assistant editor, was sabotaging him on the job. She was in her early '20s and Ali was working under her. He was 36 and felt he was getting too old for this type of work. He was depressed, his one great unconditional love, film, was betraying him.

In the summer of 1985, my wife, Roe, step-daughter, Briana and I went to England. I hadn't been home in four years so was really looking forward to the trip. Immediately after arriving, we were busy seeing relatives and friends, most of whom hadn't met my wife or step-daughter. Ali also happened to be in England at the time, but I found it difficult meeting him as he kept cancelling our arrangements. When Roe and Briana returned to America I stayed on for a few more weeks and finally managed to talk to Ali on the phone. When I informed him my family had left, he seemed upset and said, "I'm sorry Joe, I don't think I'll be able to make it after all. I'll see you back in New York." Then he hung up.

Back in New York, I called him, but his voice was even colder than it had been in England. A weirdness descended on our friendship. His new demeanour suggested he might be in serious trouble. Finally, almost eight months into June's pregnancy he officially told us she was pregnant. I congratulated him, knowing full well that he knew that I knew.

Just before Christmas, Ali came to see us in Rockaway. It was the first time we'd seen him since the Spring. He looked the same but was strangely subdued. I travelled with him to the city on Christmas Eve as he'd just found a video position on a documentary about children with AIDS and had gotten me a job on the crew as a gaffer. The shoot was at Bellevue and the director was a Spanish immigrant who, unfortunately, had adopted the worst aspects of the New World. He harangued the crew constantly, especially the camerawoman who was his wife. It was not a happy shoot. I mercifully only worked one day but Ali had two weeks more left to do.

One of the interviews we did was with a young nurse who movingly described how a child with AIDS had uttered her name with his last dying breath. She was close to tears and many in the crew, including myself, felt emotional. Except the Spaniard. After a day spent berating the entire crew, he was suddenly jovial, informing us he'd soon have the nurse in tears.

"Did you see her?" he said. "Just one more question about the boy and she would have broken down completely. I'll get her tomorrow."

The next day, I had to tape black velvet onto the wall behind the nurse to serve as a backdrop. The Spaniard arrogantly told me I hadn't taped it properly, that it would fall down. I assured him in an equally arrogant manner that it wouldn't. The videotape rolled and the Spaniard was delivering on his promise to bring the nurse to tears, which he'd said, "would make great video." Suddenly, as he teased her, the black velvet peeled off the wall behind her, ruining the entire shot. The Spaniard glared pure malice at me. I looked at Ali. His lips twitched as if he was suppressing a smile.

Afterwards I went to Ali's place and was shocked at what I found there. The once clean whitewashed walls were dirty, streaked with scuff marks and grease stains. The former home of sumptuous, fun-filled Persian delicacies was now astonishingly dingy. Then June came in. She was huge, her baby due in a week, but she was cheerful, not betraying any hint of unhappiness. Later, as Ali and I shared a cab downtown, he seemed in good spirits and as I got out we said a quick goodbye and waved at each other. For some reason, I always remember this moment as if it was a dream, a scene from a film in slow motion.

Jai was born the first week of January, a healthy

boy and Ali talked enthusiastically like the proud father he was. Then, about a month later, I got a phone call out of the blue from Ali's cousin, Clarence.

"I don't know how else to put this," he said, hesitating. "But… Ali…he's dead. He killed himself."

The previous night Ali had gotten hideously drunk mixing vodkas and brandies. He'd become so belligerent, June asked him to leave the apartment, which he did, but eventually returned. He said he was exhausted and wanted to sleep it off. Frightened, she called Clarence. But it was too late.

The funeral took place in the Bronx at a crematorium near the Museum of the American Indian. About a dozen people showed up including Clarence, Roe and myself, plus ex-NYU students. Afterwards, we went to a diner and reminisced about Ali. It relieved some of the tension and helped June bear her burden. Many of the stories were humorous. I told them about the Spaniard and the peeling tape.

There was one story I didn't tell that had happened long before. One night, after seeing a movie with June, two men rushed up behind Ali, one grabbing him by the throat and jamming the barrel of a gun against his temple.

"Make one move motherfucker and you're dead," one of them said.

They then started to frisk him roughly.

"Where is it, asshole?" they demanded.

Ali told me when the gun was put against his skull, he felt this was the end, that he was going to die. I urged him to press charges but he didn't. I later found out that Ali had stormed off the Bellevue set and some other editing jobs. I began to wonder, what was he thinking as he taped the children with AIDS documentary? Had he already made up his mind what he was going to do to himself?

CYCLING AND ME

So there I was turning the corner from Rockaway Beach Boulevard on to 130th Street on a quiet summer Sunday.

As I drove along, two cyclists came fast towards me the wrong way on a one-way and in the middle of the street. A man and a woman, oozing white middle-class respectability with impeccably matched biking outfits, they also had two carriages attached to the back of their bikes, with babies in them, which stuck out giving my car even less space to maneuver. I felt like opening my windows and yelling at them, "Are you really that stupid?" But I didn't think the children should be exposed to the fact that their parents were indeed that way.

A few weeks later I was driving to Forest Park to play tennis and on the journey home took a shortcut, avoiding Woodhaven Boulevard at rush hour all the way to Pitkin Avenue. It was late August, hot and sticky.

As I crossed Rockaway Boulevard on 85th Street, three black-clad teenagers on bikes suddenly swept in front of me. One kid, who looked to be the oldest and had a moustache, what we at home referred to as 'bum fluff,' led the threesome, which I christened 'The 85th Street Gang,' as they zigzagged from side to side, performing 'wheelies.' I didn't mind too much, I wasn't in a hurry, and hey, I was young once too. A few blocks wouldn't be too bad, but the few blocks turned into a half-mile and soon I began to get pissed. Down to 10 miles an hour and with cars lining up behind me, I started to honk my horn. All I got in return was a mean glare from the leader of the gang.

From my teaching days, I recognised his kind, one of those incorrigible little bastards angry at the world and taking it out on me.

Having taught there for a few years, I knew a Rikers Island style-homie-in training when I saw one. Rolling down my window, I appealed to one of the other kids who seemed more reasonable, asking him to move over so I could pass, adding that if I was another dude they might simply be run over. The kid smiled in a semi-friendly sort of way but then carried on exactly as before, continuing to block me.

That was it. I got really mad, cursing them loudly, "Fuck you, get out of the way, you little bastards." My poetic efforts, however, didn't have the desired effect for Mr. Mustachio suddenly braked, either hoping for a collision to set off my airbags or for compensation in case of an accident.

Mercifully, 'The 85th Street Gang' took a right turn before Pitkin Avenue. I felt like cursing them out again but refrained this time. Not out of any sense of decorum but rather because my escape route was not secure. A red light up ahead could have meant Mr. Mustachio and his mates catching up with me. It was their neighborhood, not mine, and if passing adults got involved and misunderstood the entire situation, all hell might break loose. Anything's possible in New York.

In early September, it was my turn to be a cyclist, the first time I'd being on a bike in a year.

Since my retirement from the Department of Education, I'd put on a lot of weight so I found it hard work getting on the thing and adjusting the seat to accommodate my new 'heavyweight division' status. But with pride at stake, I set off, getting as far as Riis Park.

On the way back, three Rockaway Park teenage girls cycled towards me, deliberately getting in my way, trying to throw me off balance. How had I ended up in such a precarious situation? I had done the 'Five Boro Bike Tour' five times, even avoided the Verrazzano Bridge and cycled home to Rockaway via the Coney Island Boardwalk and Brighton Beach. Probably fifty miles. I'd also cycled to Jones Beach on the Causeway and back with a friend I nicknamed Friedrich 'Superman' Nietzsche. And now here, after biking just a few blocks, were three Belle Harbor kids having a bit of fun at my expense.

Interestingly, I'd texted my wife before the

incident happened, saying, "I'm just a fat man on a fucking bike. I'm coming home." Just then, I received her response, "Yeah, but you're a handsome fucking fat man on a bike."

My wife's good like that.